A Teacher's Guide to 14–19 Policy and Practice

This concise and up-to-date guide to 14–19 education aims to demystify recent policy initiatives in the sector to help teachers and practitioners understand the rationale for the qualifications on offer and support them in their daily practice. Offering lots of additional guidance, it will help teachers to access the ongoing support that is available and develop their own professionalism.

A Teacher's Guide to 14–19 Policy and Practice considers the types of knowledge needed to teach vocational education and offers a wealth of strategies for effective learning, teaching and assessment to ensure that all students achieve and progress. It also explores the ways that teachers can follow the information, advice and guidance (IAG) standards to develop employability in the classroom and help students gain the skills they will need to manage their personal lives and careers in the future. The four sections cover:

- The political environment in 14–19 education
- Teaching and learning in the 14–19 sector
- Making 14–19 work
- Wider skills for the 14–19 practitioner

Featuring case studies, practical tasks and reflective questions, this timely new text will be essential reading for all trainee and practising teachers and practitioners in the 14–19 sector.

Lynn Senior is Dean of the College of Education at the University of Derby, UK.

A Teacher's Guide to 14–19 Policy and Practice

Lynn Senior

Routledge
Taylor & Francis Group

LONDON AND NEW YORK

First published 2017
by Routledge
2 Park Square, Milton Park, Abingdon, Oxon OX14 4RN

and by Routledge
711 Third Avenue, New York, NY 10017

Routledge is an imprint of the Taylor & Francis Group, an informa business

British Library Cataloguing in Publication Data
A catalogue record for this book is available from the British Library

Library of Congress Cataloging in Publication Data
Names: Senior, Lynn, author.
Title: A teacher's guide to 14-19 policy and practice / Lynn Senior.
Description: New York, NY : Routledge, 2016. | Includes
    bibliographical references.
Identifiers: LCCN 2016002230 | ISBN 9781138832299 (hardback) |
    ISBN 9781138832305 (pbk.) | ISBN 9781315616735 (ebook)
Subjects: LCSH: Vocational education—Great Britain. | Vocational
    teachers—Great Britain. | Effective teaching—Great Britain.
Classification: LCC LC1047.G7 S463 2016 | DDC 370.1130941—dc23
LC record available at http://lccn.loc.gov/2016002230

ISBN: 978-1-138-83229-9 (hbk)
ISBN: 978-1-138-83230-5 (pbk)
ISBN: 978-1-315-61673-5 (ebk)

Typeset in Palatino
by Swales & Willis Ltd, Exeter, Devon, UK

Contents

Tables

Figures

Acknowledgements

The author would like to thank the following:

- Alex Robinson, Lecturer at Coleg Cambria for help with Welsh 14–19 policy;
- Trevor Cox at NLT, Chesterfield for his help and advice on apprenticeships;
- Paul Senior for help with the diagrams;
- Patrick Taffin d'Heursal, Lecturer at the Swiss Education Group based in SHMS, Leysin, Switzerland for the 'flipped classroom' case study.

The political environment in 14–19 education

Policy context of 14–19 education

Introduction

14–19 education within the UK has been a much debated and contested subject over recent decades, with the 14–19 age phase being an educational stage which spanned the two traditional phases of compulsory education and post-compulsory education up until the Raising of the Participation age (RPA) in June 2015. Whilst this initiative has removed some of the confusion around 14–19, a young person at the age of sixteen can still choose to leave school to join a college, take up an apprenticeship, undertake home education or take up full-time employment, with training. It is usual to find the phrase 14–19 education linked with to the words 'vocational education' or 'education and training', which creates further debate around what 14–19 policy should look like and what its purpose should be in the UK educational framework.

The chronology of policy and initiatives leading up to the present day can provide some insight into the discussions around 14–19 and vocational education within the UK, and whilst the debates around these have been in existence for many years, this book is more concerned with how 14–19 education works in practice and the pedagogy surrounding it.

This chapter aims to situate 14–19 education within a wider policy context and discusses some of the key policy initiatives and government reports that have been introduced, removed or sidelined from vocational and 14–19 policy since the mid-1970s and those which remain influential in the 14–19 arena today.

It culminates with a brief discussion of vocational education in other countries and a comparison of their processes compared to the UK.

What is education?

General education is an umbrella term for an education that enables individuals to acquire the knowledge, skills and dispositions necessary for responsible participation in society. It has its origins in Dewey's vision for a well-rounded individual.

> *An education which acknowledges the full intellectual and social meaning of a vocation would include instruction in the historic background of present conditions; training in dealing with material and agencies of production; and study of economics, civics, and politics, to bring the future worker into touch with the problems of the day and the various methods proposed for its improvement. Above all, it would train power of re-adaptation to changing conditions so that future workers would not become blindly subject to a fate imposed upon them.*
>
> *(Dewey, 1916: 318–319)*

Therefore general education has within it the ability to reason and communicate effectively; a capacity for compassionate inquiry; a framework for intellectual, ethical and aesthetic growth; and a commitment to the wellbeing of self and the larger community.

The purpose of the general education curriculum is to prepare students to learn now and in the future world of work, in pursuit of personal fulfilment and responsible civic engagement. An educated citizen requires wide-ranging forms of knowledge. At its heart, general education embodies the concept that a well-educated student preparing for any career in the 21st century should be skilled in the following:

- inquiry and analysis;
- problem-solving and discovery;
- critical and creative thinking;
- written and oral communication;
- quantitative reasoning;
- information and technological literacy;
- teamwork and collaboration;
- ethical deliberation.

What is vocational education?

> A vocation means nothing but such a direction of life activities as renders them perceptibly significant to a person, because of the consequences they accomplish, and also useful to his associates. The opposite of a career is neither leisure nor culture but aimlessness, capriciousness, the absence of cumulative achievement in experience, on the personal side, and idle display, parasitic dependence upon the others, on the social side. Occupation is a concrete term for continuity. It includes the development of artistic capacity of any kind, of special scientific ability, of effective citizenship, as well as professional and business occupations, to say nothing of mechanical labor or engagement in gainful pursuits.
>
> (Dewey, 1916: 307)

Within this definition it can be argued that all education is fundamentally vocational, with an underlying principle of equipping young people with the skills and experiences they need to be successful in life, regardless of the country of their birth. However, the flaw in Dewey's argument is that it makes the assumption that education is progressive, and that rather than just transmitting knowledge in a traditional sense so that young people know and understand facts, the educational exchange is that of both knowledge, transmission, experience and doing. I would argue that for a curriculum to be truly vocational it has to include a mix of traditional and progressive elements and not an either/or approach. Many vocational qualifications that exist today are very much predicated on the progressive element, with an emphasis on the ability to perform tasks, rather than the underpinning knowledge of the problem which was defined by Dewey as the intellectual element of education (Ryan, 1995: 28). For example, the NVQ, introduced in the United Kingdom in 1986, had at its core, a competence-based approach, in which the learner demonstrated his or her ability to perform a set of pre-determined activities within the workplace. Whilst this qualification is still in existence within the UK framework there are several writers who believe that, as a vocational programme, the NVQ has contributed to the perception that vocational education is of less value than traditional academic education.

It is also true to say that the use of terminology such as competency, skill and training within vocational education has led to the perception that vocational education is for the less academic student and for those of a working-class status. (Lewis, 1991: 96). This can also be seen if we look at the Nuffield review, undertaken in the UK in 2009, which talks about the 'bottom half' of education (i.e. the young people who leave school and enter into the 'Not in Education, Employment or Training' (NEET) group) as those who take vocational routes.

Within the United Kingdom, the most sophisticated attempt to provide a vocational curriculum, which encompassed both vocational and general education, was the introduction of the Diploma in 2008. This qualification was to be introduced in four phases, with a total of seventeen subjects (or lines of learning) being available by 2013.

TABLE 1.1 Lines of learning

Phase	Line of learning	Year of introduction
1	Creative and Media, Engineering, IT Construction and the Built Environment, Society, Health and Development	2008
2	Environmental and Land-Based Studies Manufacturing and Product Design Hospitality, Hair and Beauty Studies Business, Administration and Finance	2009
3	Public Services, Sport and Leisure Travel and Tourism, Retail	2010
4	Humanities, Sciences, Languages	2011

(Senior, 2010: 6)

They were to be introduced at three levels, Level 1 – Foundation (equivalent to 5 GCSEs D–G), Level 2 – Higher (equivalent to 7 GCSEs A*–C) and Level 3 – Advanced (equivalent to 2.5 A levels).

As per the themes presented by Tomlinson (2004) each diploma was designed to enable progression into either higher level qualifications or employment.

The qualification was formed from three distinct components.

These distinct components were further broken down as:

- Principal learning: developing knowledge, understanding and skills in the context of a particular sector;

- Generic learning, including functional skills in English, Maths and IT, and personal learning and thinking skills;

- Additional/specialist learning, which offers young people the opportunity to study a particular topic in more depth or broaden their studies through complementary learning. This element also allowed a young person to create a qualification that was unique and individualised to their own specific career choice.

- Work experience was a key feature of all diplomas, with a minimum of 10 days needed; and

- Extended project: the Diploma at Level 3 included an extended project to allow individuals to plan and organise their own learning and demonstrate project management, synthesis and other higher skills that universities and employers need.

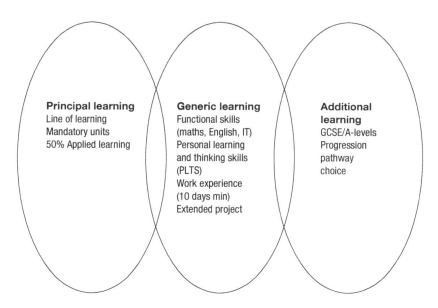

FIGURE 1.1 The components of the Diploma

(Senior, 2010: 7)

Harkin described the Diploma as a qualification whereby:

■ *Students are challenged to think, to develop in-depth understanding, and to apply academic learning to important, real-world problems.*

■ *Pedagogy must include connections to the World Beyond the Classroom.*

■ *Assessment Tasks must include problems connected to the world and an audience beyond the School.*

(Harkin, 2008: 17)

However, this qualification was short lived and following the 2010 election it disappeared from the UK framework.

The debate about the relative benefits of general versus vocational education is often framed by the contrast between the American and European systems of education. Whereas the United States emphasises formal general education in secondary schools, much of Europe relies on vocational training and apprenticeships to prepare its workforce for the labour market.

Chronology of 14–19 policy

The latter half of the 20th century saw high and rising employment and the decline of traditional manufacturing industries.

I would suggest that the current thinking around vocational education can be traced back to the Callaghan's Ruskin speech, often referred to as the 'Great Debate' of 1976, where concerns around specialisation at A-Level plus the lack of skills within the curriculum were initially raised by the then Labour government.

Several initiatives followed the 1976 speech:

- The Holland Report (1977);
- A New Training Initiative (1981);
- 17+: A New Qualification (1982);
- TVEI (1982);
- YTS (1983);
- Training for Jobs White Paper (1984);
- The establishment of the National Certificate in Vocational Qualifications (NCVQ) in 1986, which introduced the competence-based NVQs, which were qualifications based in the workplace.

These initiatives were designed to build a better workforce and provide skills and training to prepare young people for the world of work. In the mid-1970s, a pilot scheme of vocational preparation was launched aimed at 16-year-olds entering into employment without training. This initiative was the precursor to the Technical and Vocational Education Initiative (TVEI), introduced by Margaret Thatcher in 1983 to 'provide a full-time programme, offer a progressive four-year course combining general with technical and vocational education, commence at 14 years; be broadly based; include planned work experience; lead to nationally recognised qualifications' (MSC, 1984, quoted in Dale, 1990: 13). The TVEI initiative represents the first time that the concept of the 14–19 age phase is suggested in the UK discourse.

Two reports, *A British Baccalaureate: Ending the Division Between Education and Training* (Institute of Public Policy, 1990) and *Education and Training for the 21st Century* (DES, 1991), focused on an attempt to bridge the gap between vocational and academic education and qualifications. The former report proposed a unitary advanced diploma that would be delivered through the tertiary colleges, whilst the latter argued that 'young people should not have their opportunities limited by out-of-date distinctions between qualifications' (DES 1991: 58). These two reports were quickly followed in the early 1990s by a further series of initiatives centred on vocational education and training (VET) and the skills agenda, for example the introduction of GNVQs in 1992, based in colleges, not the workplace. This qualification was designed to relate to occupational areas rather than specific jobs and was an attempt to combine work-based learning with a core academic curriculum to provide the underpinning knowledge of the broader occupational base. It was offered in both schools and colleges, but more commonly in colleges or as post-16 one-year courses for students who wished to continue post-GCSE but were not A-Level standard. It was introduced in 1992 and came to an end in 2007.

The 14–19 educational phase

I would like to start with some discussion around the importance of 14–19 as an educational phase. As previously mentioned, the raising of the participation age (RPA) to 17 in 2013, and to 18 in 2015 created the need for all young people to remain in education or training leading to a recognised qualification. In addition, the age of 14–19 is seen as a period of transition between education and adult working life and the policy initiatives that have been in place around this phase have all had at their core a need to improve the skills, attainment and progression of young people into the world of work. However, despite all of the policy initiatives and discussion, the '14–19' phase, whilst existing in law does not appear to be championed as well as it perhaps should be, and indeed current government thinking prefers 14–16/16–18 divisions (Skills Commission 2014). Hence, maybe leading to some of the confusion, challenge and contradictions around the 14–19 learner and their educational needs. Over the last few years the UK government has been committed to ensuring that our young people are better educated, better trained and highly skilled as a workforce. This in turn has led to 14–19 as an age phase having a variety of socio-economic and political goals in addition to the goals of the individual learner, leading to potential issues of balance between competing goals of the stakeholders. So, it could be questioned whether the main purpose of 14–19 education is purely economic. Within this stage your learners will be facing major changes as they develop as young adults and with that develop their own individuality and behaviours. One of the key requirements for the 14–19 educator is to understand and track the progress of these learners, who will have a wide range of aspirations, prior achievements and indeed personalities.

Some individuals within this phase may choose the traditional academic track of A-levels leading to further study in higher education. Others may feel that a college-based or apprenticeship route is more suited to their learning style and aspirations, and whilst this may still lead them into higher education, the route and the pedagogy required will be very different for the 14–19 educator. What is clear is that there are many options available to the 14–19 cohort and a myriad of qualifications that they can choose from. The next section will briefly discuss the chronology leading to the current environment, and whilst not intended to be a complete history, it will highlight some of the key policies and government reports that have shaped 14–19 education.

In the UK the traditional key stage 4 provision for 14–16 year olds was subject to the National Curriculum requirements, which established a number of compulsory subjects that a 14–16 year old should study., These three compulsory aspects to the National Curriculum are core subjects, plus entitlement and vocational elements. The 16–19 provision in the UK was used to denote specialist provision, be that academic qualifications in the form of A-levels, vocational qualifications, or work-based training. As a sector 14–19 has always been a mismatch to the traditional 14–16 and 16–19 phases, and whilst several initiatives have targeted 14–19, the concept of it as a specific phase has always had blurred lines. The raising of the participation age (RPA) to 17 in 2013 and 18 in 2015, has also created confusion about what 14–19 actually is and what it means for qualifications.

A brief history of qualifications

As previously discussed the policies that surround the 14–19 age phase and the ensuing qualifications are numerous. This section aims to provide the reader with an overview of some of the more significant programmes that were developed and that may still have relevance and learning for today's qualification offer.

The Technical and Vocational Education Initiative (TVEI) and the General National Vocational qualification (GNVQ) introduced in 1982 and 1991 respectively were two of the vocational programmes designed to promote vocational education and training aimed at students in full-time education.

The introductions of TVEI and GNVQ were separated by less than ten years and operationally the two programmes overlapped within many schools and colleges. However, there were very significant differences in the ways in which TVEI and GNVQ set about tackling deficiencies in vocational education for the 14–19 age group. Both of the programmes were developed to improve what was perceived as low-quality vocational education, with a remit to provide vocational skills to help improve the UK economic standing by aligning education more closely to the needs of industry, through providing skills and knowledge to enable the school leaver to be work ready. This discussion around skills deficit has been a common thread throughout vocational education as you will see when we look at other qualifications that have been and gone. TVEI was a political intervention to make use of surplus funds in the MSC. However, as with many vocational initiatives and qualifications it was susceptible to shifts in party politics and the DES (1987) discussion paper which introduced the National Curriculum was in many ways the final nail in the coffin.

As a contrast the GNVQ was developed to provide a broader-based education that had within it specific competencies. Similar to the National Vocational Qualification (NVQ), it was less reliant on the workplace as much of the competency could be assessed in the school or college, through role play, simulation of work experience, drawing upon the application of theory to practice.

The final report of the working group on 14–9 qualifications and curriculum reform, more commonly referred to as the 'Tomlinson Report' was published in 2004. This report had at its core an overarching qualification, the 14–19 Diploma, combining both academic and vocational qualifications, with an aim to raise the standards and esteem of vocational education within the UK. The report recognised that all children should be given the opportunity to achieve and that no one size fits all:

> Every young person is different, so they should not all have to study the same mix of subjects at school or college. We propose up to 20 different subject mixes through which young people can gain their diploma. Young people could choose an 'open' diploma with a mix of subjects similar to those taken by many GCSE and A level

students today. Alternatively they could choose a diploma specialising in an employment sector or academic discipline. Students might opt for an engineering diploma, a languages and literature diploma or a science and mathematics diploma, for example. 14–16 year olds would continue to study National Curriculum subjects, though their diploma would not depend on achieving a specific grade in those subjects. All students under 16 would take open diplomas to avoid narrowing their options too soon.

(DfES,2004: 4).

This proposal was the first of its kind and as a concept an overarching 14–19 Diploma was unique in that it straddled two sectors of education: 14–16 and 16+. In doing so it created a need for collaboration between schools, colleges and employers in order to implement the qualification effectively. It truly embodied a 14–19 phase.

The report proposed that the new qualification should replace the existing qualifications of GCSE, A and A/S levels plus the range of BTEC and AVCE qualifications. However, despite support from many in education, the government response to the report was to reject the proposal of an overarching qualification and reform the existing qualifications.

In 2005 the *14–19 Education and Skills* bill announced a watered down version of the proposals put forward by Tomlinson and announced the introduction of a new 14–19 vocational diploma, later to be renamed the Diploma, which would sit alongside existing qualifications.

Following the introduction of the first three phases of Diploma subjects, the coalition government (formed in 2010) removed all support and funding for the Diploma. This action was followed by a review of all vocational education, undertaken by Alison Wolf (2011). This review effectively removed over 2000 qualifications from the qualifications framework.

Current provision in 14–19 education

As we moved post-2012, the coalition government did not appear to support the 14–19 phase, and following the 2011 Wolf Review of vocational education over 3000 vocational qualifications were removed from the school performance league tables. Some academics noted that 'the piecemeal approach to 14–19 education and training appears to be back', as discussed by (Higham and Yeomans, 2007: 221).

To add more complexity to the idea of the 14–19 phase it was announced by the Skills Minister, Matthew Hancock, in December 2013 that certain vocational qualifications had met the required standards to be included in schools and college performance tables and would be available from September 2014. In addition, he announced two new types of vocational qualifications for 16–19 year olds, those being Tech Levels and Applied General qualifications. In addition, in 2013, the Government issued information on reforming the further education system. This reform was designed to ensure that further education colleges provided high-quality vocational teaching and education leading to employment. As part of this initiative it introduced new funding for people aged 24+ studying at Levels 3 and 4 or for higher or advanced apprenticeships, and in addition reformed the funding and content for 16–18 provision through the introduction of study programmes. These programmes have now been introduced in both schools and colleges and include a mixture of general and vocational learning. The initiative also included proposals for improving and reforming the apprenticeship system and bestowed power upon colleges to enrol 14–16 year olds as part of its student population.

Study programmes

Following Professor Alison Wolf's review of vocational education (Wolf, 2011) the recommendation was that there was a need to meet the needs of the labour market through a study programme that incorporated vocational qualifications together with GCSE in English and Maths where learners had not achieved grade C or above.

At the time of writing the government agenda seems to have gone back to the traditional post-16 and pre-16 phases of learning rather than the 14–19 phase as the previous administration appeared to favour and as the development of UTC (as discussed earlier) would suggest.

> *Young people in this age group are very different in their interests and ambitions. Unlike 14–16 year olds, it is appropriate that they should be offered a wide range of specialist options, and programmes which are highly diverse rather than dominated by a large common core. These cannot be designed and dictated centrally. They need to be developed by colleges, schools and providers, in response to the interests and ambitions of their clientele. The government's proposals, including, crucially, its proposed funding reforms, are designed to enable innovation and responsiveness to local needs and demand. I look forward to watching the post-16 sector develop high-quality and diverse programmes for this age group in the years ahead*
>
> *(Wolf, 2011: 4)*

The report also makes a recommendation that schools and colleges be encouraged to prioritise longer high-quality internships or placements for 16–19 year olds, reflecting the fact that almost no young people move into full-time employment at 16. The proposal for Study Programmes was accepted for implementation for colleges, private providers and state funded schools in 2013 and coincided with new funding streams.

Visit the website for more information on the 16–19 Study Programmes www. tinyurl.com/qj4t2th

---

Activity

Consider the offering in your institution. What makes up the Study Programme for your learners?

Apprenticeships 14–19

The National Apprenticeship Service, part of the Skills Funding Agency, is the government agency that co-ordinates apprenticeships in England, enabling young people to enter the skilled trades. At the beginning of February 2008 the Labour Government published a document called 'Strategy for the Future of Apprenticeships in England'. Apprenticeships are demand-led, funded by the Government, in full for 16 to 19-year-olds and in part for adults, but rely on employers and providers to work together to offer sufficient opportunities in the context of the greater freedoms and flexibilities created in the further education system. Therefore, Government does not plan apprenticeship places but provides funding and forecasts the number of places that may be afforded as a result. By 2022, two million more jobs will require higher-level skills, according to last year's 'Forging Futures' report by the UK Commission for Employment.

With an ageing population, accompanied by growth in health and social care sectors and a decrease in construction and agricultural industries, there's never been a better time to look at filling those skill gaps. Apprenticeships, higher apprenticeships and degree apprenticeships are now all part of the government agenda for improving skills.

The Department for Business, Innovation and Skills has announced its commitment to create three million apprenticeship starts by 2020 and will work closely with colleges and business to make sure it happens. Ultimately, the aim is to increase the skills of our workforce and increase productivity across the country.

Strategies have also been put into place to rebrand vocational education, including the provision of state-of-the-art facilities, engaging in more research activities and collaborating on the design and development of apprenticeship programmes with employers.

Many of the skills most needed to compete in the global market of the 21st century are technical skills that fall into the vocational area, and the government suggests that the absence of excellence in many technical and vocational fields is costing us economically as a nation. For vocational education to be effective there also needs to be a much stronger emphasis on practical skills and working with the employer.

There are potentially huge benefits to the employer and the apprentice. Businesses are much more likely to be able to meet their needs by recruiting from a much larger talent pool, which will in turn increase productivity, fill skills gaps and enable them to develop existing staff.

For the apprentices, the advantages are clear: being able to combine on-the-job vocational training with academic qualifications, gain professional accreditation and membership, have no debt at the end of the programme and be more likely to have a clear pathway for their career goals.

As with the Study Programmes, young people can start an apprenticeship at the age of 16, although they can apply from the age of 14. Apprenticeships combine practical training in a job with study. As an apprentice the learner will work alongside experienced staff to gain job-specific skills. They will earn a wage and also study towards a related qualification, normally one day a week in a further education college. Apprenticeships take one to four years to complete depending on their level.

Levels of apprenticeship

An apprenticeship has an equivalent education level and can be:

■ intermediate – equivalent to five GCSE passes;

■ advanced – equivalent to two A-level passes;

■ higher – can lead to NVQ Level 4 and above, or a foundation degree.

At the time of writing several 'trailblazer' projects are in existence that are seeking to develop apprenticeships at levels 6 and 7. Trailblazers are groups of employers that have been leading the way in carrying out the changes to apprenticeships. They have been working together to design apprenticeship standards and assessment approaches to make them world class. (See www.gov.uk/government/publications/future-of-apprenticeships-in-england-guidance-for-trailblazers)

Other qualifications available for the 14–19 student

The list below provides some indication of programmes and course types available to the 14–19 learner, and whilst not exhaustive, it gives an indication of the current offer.

■ Entry Level Diploma

■ Foundation Diploma

■ Diploma

■ Extended Diploma

■ BTEC First Certificate

■ BTEC National Certificate

■ NVQ

Activity

Look at your organisation and the types of programmes they offer. What are the major differences and levels between the different programmes?

14–19 in other UK Countries

Much of what has already been discussed is relevant to the English system only as the three other countries within the UK have their own 14–19 agenda and policy. This next section will briefly consider those policies and any implications for the learner.

14–19 Education in Scotland

The Commission for Developing Scotland's Young Workforce was set up in January 2013 to with the following three aims:

- Create a high-quality intermediate vocational education and training system that can be developed to enhance sustainable economic growth with a skilled workforce.
- Achieve connectivity and cooperation between education and the world of work to ensure young people at all levels of education understand the expectations of employers, and that employers are properly engaged.
- Achieve a culture of real partnership between employers and education, where employers view themselves as co-investors and co-designers rather than simply customers.

These aims resonate with the overall goals within the English system in that the aspiration is for a highly qualified workforce that can promote economic growth. It could be suggested that, based on this, the 14–19 system in Scotland has the same issues that the English system faces, not least the potential difference in aspirations and goals between the government as a key stakeholder and the young person entering into 14–19 education.

In implementation terms the Scottish system is very similar to that of England in that it sets out a number of recommendations for vocational education: school based, college based and workplace/apprenticeship based.

Recommendations for schools

The report produced by the commission has two recommendations for school-based education. Firstly, that industry-based qualifications should sit alongside academic qualifications and where practical should be developed in consultation and partnership with colleges. Secondly, a focus on preparing all young people for employment should form a core element of the implementation of Curriculum for Excellence with appropriate resource dedicated to achieve this. In particular local authorities, Skills Development Scotland and employer representative organisations should work together to develop a more comprehensive standard for careers guidance which would reflect the involvement of employers and their role and input.

The role of the colleges in Scotland is focussed on employment outcomes and supporting local economic development. This should be underpinned by eleven meaningful and wide-ranging partnerships with industry and should be at the fore-front of Regional Outcome Agreements and their measurement.

14–19 Wales

On 29 September 2011 the Deputy Minister for Skills, Jeff Cuthbert, launched a review to look into the qualifications currently on offer. The aims were to identify the qualifications that are most relevant, valued and understood and to ensure that these are available to learners. It also considered issues related to assess-ment and measurement of performance. The review ran from September 2011 to November 2012.

The review was overseen by a project board consisting of external advisers and internal Welsh Government officials, with an external Chair. This ensured that the review was based on impartial views and evidence, and was open to ideas and challenge from stakeholders.

The project board delivered its final report and recommendations to the Deputy Minister for Skills on 28 November 2012. In January 2013, the Deputy Minister made an oral statement announcing that the Welsh Government broadly accepted all of the review's recommendations. In September 2015 the Welsh Government is set to completely reform the education system for 14 to 19 year olds in Wales.

This agenda for change is the result of the extensive evidence-based research con-ducted for the compilation of the 'Review of Qualifications for 14 to 19-year-olds in Wales', an independent report conducted in 2012 on behalf of the Welsh Government. The purpose of this Review was to establish whether qualifications in Wales were 'meeting the needs of our young people and the economy' (www.qualifiedforlife. org.uk/). It concluded that,

> The time has come to develop a high quality, robust and distinctive national qualifi-cations system for 14 to 19-year-olds in Wales . . . a large proportion of qualifications will continue to be shared with England . . . However, decisions about qualifications in Wales must be taken in a strategic way and on what is best for our learners and our economy.
>
> (Review of Qualifications 14 to 19-year-olds, 21996, p. 4).

However, although the conclusion of the Review states the importance of 'creat-ing divergence between Wales and other parts of the UK' (Review of Qualifications 14 to 19-year-olds, 2012, p.4), in the same paragraph it claims 'there may be scope for closer working alignment with Scotland, Northern Ireland and Europe'. (Review of

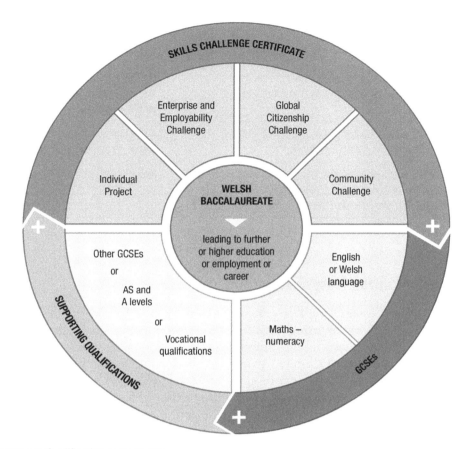

FIGURE 1.2 Qualification components

(Adapted from Welsh Government, 2015)

Qualifications 14 to 19-year-olds, 2012, p.4). I am not a geography teacher, however I am assured that Scotland and Northern Ireland are part of the UK.

The Review board identified twelve underpinning principles for 14–19 education in Wales, one of which was that the revised Welsh Baccalaureate (WBQ) would be at the heart of the new system. The Review proposes that the WBQ will provide the overarching framework for the entire qualifications system for 14–19 year olds.

In Wales the approach taken is similar to that in England, with a 14–19 pathway approach. This focuses on the needs of individual learners and their learning experience – formal, non-formal and informal education – and the development of skills which will help them to achieve their potential.

The learning pathways framework consists of six key elements. Some are unique to Wales and fall into two distinct categories: learner provision and learner support. These elements are identified in the following table:

TABLE 1.2 Learner provision and learner support

Learner provision	Learner support
Individual learning pathway – to meet the needs of each individual, including formal, non-formal and informal strands.	Access to learning coach – support for learning to be available at greater intensity for those in greatest need.
Wider choice and flexibility of courses – leading to qualifications from a local curriculum.	Access to personal support – to help overcome personal barriers to learning.
Wider learning from the learning core – including skills, knowledge, attitudes values and experiences that all 14 to 19 year olds will need, whatever their pathway.	Impartial careers advice and guidance.

Adapted from www.wales.gov.uk/topics/educationandskills/pathways

14–19 Education Northern Ireland

In Northern Ireland the Department of Education (DE) and the Department for Employment and Learning (DEL) work closely together on cross-cutting issues related to the education and training provision for 14–19 year olds. The departments have a shared focus on young people having access to the right courses; on quality teaching and learning; on careers provision; on helping young people avoid being part of the Not in Employment, Education or Training (NEETs) statistics; and STEM.

Both departments are determined to enhance the contribution of schools, further education, higher education and training to the development of the local economy.

The Entitlement Framework in Northern Ireland

The Entitlement Framework is the post-14 curriculum which puts the needs of pupils first. It aims to provide access for pupils to a broad and balanced curriculum to enable them to reach their full potential no matter which school they attend or where they live.

It will guarantee all pupils access to a minimum number of courses at Key Stage 4 and post-16, of which at least one third must be general and one third applied. The Department for Education will specify the number of courses and is responsible for designating courses as general or applied.

For further information on the legislation and entitlement visit www.nidirect. gov.uk/articles/education-14-19-year-olds www.deni.gov.uk/index/curriculum-and-learningt-new/curriculum-and-assessment-2/entitlement-framework.htm# whatisit.

Vocational education globally

The first part of this chapter explored and discussed 14–19 policy and vocational education within the UK educational system. This final section will start to examine other countries and how they have developed vocational education in comparison to the UK. Most educational systems around the world contain both a general and a vocational component of secondary schooling. However, there is remarkable diversity in the emphasis on general versus vocational education across different countries and a long-standing debate about the relative benefits of vocational versus general education.

Vocational education In Europe

Within Europe the European Commission publish 'The Education and Training Monitor', an annual series that reports on the evolution of education and training systems across Europe. The Education and Training Monitor supports the implementation of the strategic framework for European co-operation in education and training (known as ET 2020) by strengthening the evidence-base and by linking it more closely to the broader Europe 2020 strategy and the country-specific recommendations (CSRs) adopted by the commission as part of the 2014 European Semester.

The third annual edition of the Education and Training Monitor was published in November 2014.

Activity

Go to the website and read the Education and Training Monitor November 2014. What implications could this report have for you and your organisation? www.ec.europa.eu/education/library/publications/monitor14_en.pdf

---

The role of the EU in VET

The Directorate General for Education and Culture (DG EAC) is the branch of the European Commission charged with education and training. Its activities are framed by the Education and Training 2020 strategy (ET 2020), and as a part of the Europe 2020 strategy, it is designed to promote growth and jobs in Europe, as well as contributing to the development of skills for the labour market.

DG EAC is responsible for the development and management of initiatives to support education and training across Europe. One of the most well-known initiatives is the Erasmus + Programme.

Since 2010, with the approval of the Europe 2020 strategy, a variety of initiatives have been launched including:

■ Youth on the Move (YotM), whose aim is to help better equip young people for the job market – which includes boosting the literacy of the less skilled – and to improve their education and training levels.

■ The Agenda for new skills and jobs, which includes literacy as an important part of the right mix of skills needed for success in the future labour market.

■ The Digital Agenda for Europe, which recognises the role of digital literacy for empowerment and participation in the digital era.

■ The European Platform against Poverty and Social Exclusion, which proposes the development of innovative education for deprived communities to help lift them out of poverty and social exclusion.

These initiatives have resulted in the following actions:

■ The Rethinking Education initiative;

■ The establishment of the Alliance of Apprenticeships;

■ The communication on modernisation of higher education;

■ The Opening up Education initiative;

■ The Education and Training Monitor, and co-operation with surveys such as the Programme for International Student Assessment (PISA) and Programme for the International Assessment of Adult Competencies (PIAAC).

The next section provides a brief overview of some of the vocational education and training systems across Europe.

Vocational education in Switzerland

The majority of vocational education in Switzerland follows a dual-track system, part-time classroom based and part-time in the workplace in an apprenticeship with a host company. Currently Switzerland has over 250 programmes that students can choose from. There is a very small minority of vocational education that is provided solely in the classroom, mainly career or trade schools. Switzerland also offers a Professional Education and Training route (PET) system.

Within Switzerland VET is provided at upper-secondary level. Professional educational training (PET) is provided at tertiary B level. Both VET and PET use clearly defined curricula and national qualification procedures. They are also characterised by a high degree of permeability: a credit system to keep track of prior education and training makes it much easier for learners to pursue additional education and training opportunities and change the course of their working lives.

Activity

For a visual overview of the Swiss system visit the following web adress.
www.tinyurl.com/qdobwut
How could this system be adapted for the UK?

Vocational education in Finland

The VET sector in Finland comprises upper-secondary vocational education and training and further vocational training. It is targeted towards both young people ready to enter the labour market and adults already in gainful employment or outside the labour market. In addition to providing students with diverse knowledge, skills and competence required to enter and function in the world of work, vocational education and training prepares students for lifelong learning and self-development. Education and training can be organised diversely both in institutional learning environments and in workplaces as well as using online learning environments.

Upper-secondary vocational education and training covers upper-secondary vocational qualifications and various pre-vocational programmes preparing students for upper-secondary vocational studies. Further vocational training includes further and specialist qualifications as well as further training not leading to any specific qualification, organised according to the needs of individual students and employers.

In Finland, vocational adult education and training is very much based on the system of competence-based qualifications. A specific benefit of this system is that it makes it possible to recognise an individual's vocational competencies regardless of whether they were acquired through work experience, studies or other activities.

The following link provides more information on the Finnish system: www.tinyurl.com/z2fmy92

Vocational education in Germany

Vocational education and training in Germany is a joint government–industry programme. The federal government and the *Laender* share in the financing of vocational education in public vocational schools, with the federal government bearing a slightly higher share (58 per cent in 1991) than the *Laender*. On-the-job vocational training, whose cost is entirely borne by companies and businesses, is more costly to provide than vocational education. In the early 1990s, companies and businesses annually spent 2 per cent of their payrolls on training.

Within Germany, vocational education and training is deeply embedded and widely respected. It is a dual system that integrates work-based and school-based learning to prepare apprentices for a successful transition to full-time employment. One of the major strengths of the German system and a clear reason for its success is the high level of engagement and ownership on the part of employers and other social partners. However, the system also has within it an intricate web of checks and balances at the national, state, municipal, and company levels that ensures that the short-term needs of employers do not distort broader educational and economic goals. In addition Germany has a well-developed and institutionalised VET research capacity, including the Federal Institute for VET, (*BIBB*), and a national network of research centres that study different aspects of the system to support continuous innovation and improvement in the VET system. All of which continue to ensure its success.

Building upon the junior secondary program, the *Berufsschulen* are two- and three-year vocational schools that prepare young people for a profession. *Berufsschulen*, also called intermediate technical schools (ITS). These schools usually offer full-time vocation-specific programs. They are attended by students who want to train for a specialty or those already in the workforce who want to earn the equivalent of an intermediate school certificate from a *Realschule*. Full-time programmes take between 12 and 18 months, and part-time programs take between three and three and a half years. Other types of schools designed to prepare students for different kinds of vocational careers are the higher technical schools (HTS), the *Fachoberschule*, and the advanced vocational school (AVS).

Vocational education worldwide

The next section will look at some of the other countries across the world and explore how they do VET. Whilst not an exhaustive list, I have tried to identify countries that are perceived to do well with vocational education and have robust systems, policies and practices surrounding VET.

Vocational education in the United States

In the United States, vocational education varies from state to state, with much being provided through private 'career schools'. Federal involvement in vocational education is carried out through the Carl D. Perkins Vocational and Technical Education Act, first introduced in 1984 and re-established in 2006 as the Carl D. Perkins Career and Technical Education Improvement Act. This act provides funding from the federal government for vocational education across all of the US.

Vocational education in New Zealand

New Zealand has a range of initiatives in place to support vocational education. Technical and Vocational Education and Training (TVET) begins at school and with schools' arrangements with tertiary providers. Tertiary TVET is offered at Institutes of Technology and Polytechnics (ITPs), Industry Training Organisations (ITOs),

Wānanga, Private Training Establishments (PTEs) and in the workplace. Some programmes are also available in government training establishments and several universities.

Trades academies

At the time of writing there are currently 22 trades academies run through schools and other providers that deliver trades and technology programmes to students in Years 11 to 13 (ages 15 to 18). These take account of local and national workforce needs, and are aligned to allow students to achieve secondary and tertiary qualifications. Trades may include such areas as tourism, primary industries, building and construction, hospitality, engineering, business, computing, and more.

Institutes of Technology and Polytechnics (ITP)

Currently there are 18 Institutes of Technology and Polytechnics (ITPs) in New Zealand. They provide professional and vocational education and training on a wide range of subjects from introductory studies through to full degree programmes.

Programmes are at all levels: community interest courses, English language training, foundation programmes, certificates, diplomas, degrees and some postgraduate qualifications. The most common qualifications ITPs award are certificates and diplomas, encouraging students to build from lower qualifications to higher ones.

Courses emphasise practical experience and application to work situations such as studios, workshops, laboratories, hospitals and other workplaces.

Industry Training Organisations (ITO)

New Zealand has around 20 Industry Training Organisations (ITOs). These are government- and industry-funded bodies that represent particular industry sectors. They develop and maintain national standards and qualifications for their sector. They also facilitate on-the-job training and contract training providers to offer off-the-job training and courses.

Private Training Establishments (PTE)

Many of New Zealand's Private Training Establishments (PTEs) offer specific vocational niches at certificate and diploma level for occupations. At any one time there are approximately 600 registered Private Training Establishments (PTEs), including registered private English language schools.

Vocational education in Australia

Australia's VET sector is based on a partnership between governments and industry. VET qualifications are provided by government institutions, called technical and further education (TAFE) institutions, as well as private institutions.

Australian governments (federal and state) provide funding, develop policies, and contribute to regulation and quality assurance of the sector. Industry and employer groups contribute to training policies and priorities, and in developing qualifications that deliver skills to the workforce.

Vocational education in South Africa

Prior to 2000, there were 33 industry training boards in South Africa that covered various sectors in the country. While their responsibility was supposedly 'education and training', they focused mainly on apprenticeships. In 1998, the South African Parliament ratified the Skills Development Act which defined a new Sector Training and Education Authority (SETA) system. In essence, the plan was to develop a series of sector skills plans within a clearly defined framework of the National Skills Development Strategy.

In March 2000, the then Minister of Labour, Membathisi Mdladlana formally established 23 SETAs, each with its own clearly defined sector and sub-sectors. Each of the sectors was made up of a variety of economic activities that were related and closely linked. Unlike the old training boards, the SETAs were to be concerned with learnerships, internships, unit-based skills programmes and apprenticeships.

One of the primary objectives of the SETAs was to collect skills levies from employers within each sector, in terms of the Skills Development Levies Act, and make the money available within the sector for education and training.

In November 2009, the Department of Higher Education and Training announced that it would assume responsibility for skills development and proposed a new SETA landscape and a draft framework for a new National Skills Development Strategy to be implemented between March 2011 and March 2016.

Conclusion

This chapter set out to explore some of the different vocational policies across Europe and further afield. It is not an exhaustive exploration of vocational policy, but provides an overview of some of the countries that are perceived to 'do VET properly'.

Activity

You may wish to take some time to explore vocational practices and 14–19 teaching in other countries such as Finland, Sweden and Germany, all of whom have very strongly embedded practice. How could the United Kingdom learn from the way that they approach things? Could any good practice be shared to enhance either country?

14–19 Education as a concept is not new. However, it is a concept that is consumed by challenge, change and confusion, not least because of the perceptions of the vocational education agenda within the current UK government, with the learner and other stakeholders. The next section of the book will start to examine vocational pedagogy and 14–19 practice that as a practitioner, whether a teacher, lecturer, assessor or work-based mentor, you may find useful in your daily practice.

Reflecting on practice

After reading this chapter you should be aware of some of the differences in VET across a range of different countries. There are a number of areas you may wish to consider as a practitioner to support the development of VET in the UK.

- How can you engage the workforce to support vocational education more effectively?
- How can you 'make it real' for the learner, work-placements, work-related and work-based options
- What is the role of the government and how they should support VET within the United Kingdom?

References

Dale, R. (1990) *The TVEI Story: Policy, Practice and Preperation for the Workforce*. Milton Keynes: Open University Press.

Dearing, R. (1996) *Review of Qualifications for 16-19 Year Olds* (Dearing II). Hayes: SCAA.

DES (1987) *The National Curriculum*. HMSO: London.

DES (1991) *Education and Training for the 21st Century*. London: HMSO.

Dewey, J. (1916) *Democracy and Education*. New York: Touchstone.

DfES (1997) *The Dearing Report: Higher Education in the Learning Society*. London: HMSO.

DfES, (2004). *14–19 Curriculum and Qualifications Reform: Final Report of the Working Group on 14–19 Reform*. London: DfES.

Harkin, J. (2008) *Excellence in Supporting Applied Learning: Professional Development for the 14–19 Curriculum in the School and FE Sectors* (presentation). London: TDA/LLUK.

Higham, J. & Yeomans, D. (2007). 'Curriculum choice, flexibility and differentiation 14–19: the way forward or flawed prospectus?', *London Review of Education*, 5 (3): 281–297.

Institute of Public Policy (1990) *A British Baccalaureate: Ending the Division Between Education and Training*. London: IPPR.

Lewis, T. (1991) 'Difficulties attending the new vocationalism in the USA', *Journal of Philosophy of Education*, Wiley online library.

Ryan, A. (1995) *John Dewey and the High Tide of American Liberalism*. New York: Norton.

Senior, L. (2010) *The Essential Guide to Teaching 14–19 Diplomas*. London: Pearson.

Skills Commission (2014) www.gov.uk/government/organisations/uk-commission-for-employment-and-skills (accessed March 2016).

Tomlinson, M. (2004) *14–19 Curriculum and Qualifications Reform: Final Report of the Working Group on 14-19 Reform*. London: DfE-0976-2004.

Wolf, A. (2011) *A Review of Vocational Education – The Wolf Report*. London: DfE.

Welsh Government, (2015), *Qualified for Life*. Available from http://qualifiedforlife. org.uk/ (accessed 1 March, 2015.)

Further reading

Department for Education, Lifelong Learning and Skills, Welsh Assembly Government (2001) *The Learning Country: Vision into Action*. Available from www.gov.wales/dcells/publications/publications/guidanceandinformation/ learningcountry/learningcountryvis-e.pdf?lang=en (accessed 5 March, 2015.)

Qualifications and Learning Division Department for Education and Skills Welsh Government, (2012) *Review of Qualifications for 14 to 19-Year-Olds in Wales*. Available from www.gov.wales/docs/dcells/publications/121127reviewofqualificationsen. pdf (accessed 28 February, 2015.)

Stenlund, T. (2010), 'Assessment of prior learning in higher education: A review from a validity perspective', *Assessment & Evaluation In Higher Education*, 35, 7: 783–797.

Teaching and learning in the 14–19 sector

2

Social and emotional development of the 14–19 learner

Learning objectives

After studying this chapter you will be able to:

- define social and emotional development;
- apply theories of social and emotional development to the 14–19 age phase;
- discuss the concept of social learning;
- consider how motivation plays a part in learning;
- consider classroom and teaching strategies to support the 14–19 learner.

Introduction

Understanding how children and adolescents develop is a crucial factor in comprehending how learners learn and make progress.

There are many individuals that will influence a child's development from 0–19 including parents, carers, childcare workers, and teachers, as well as the child's own peer group. Learning in one phase of development underpins and enables learning in the next. Within the 14–19 age group the students will have already been subjected to many influences that affect or could affect their attainment, whether that be the childcare provision received, classroom teaching or just simply parental engagement.

For you as the teacher any problems within the earlier phases could manifest as a wide range of different physical, cognitive and social and emotional needs. The main task is to identify things that can be remediated to help everyone fulfil their own potential.

This chapter will explore the social and emotional development of the 14–19 learner and examine strategies that could be used to support their learning.

Social learning

All learning takes place within social spheres that can inform, develop, influence and have a major impact upon the individual. Cooley (1909) identified three main groups that can influence learning: family, peers and community.

Family

14–19 learners' experiences and social relationships are developed in the family setting. Values and experiences at this stage are important as children model their family members. In today's society some of our young people may come from one-parent families. Whilst this in itself may not be of detriment to the young person it can have a bearing on their prior knowledge and experiences. A colleague of mine works with trainee electricians, and he is adamant that he can tell those who have grown up without a male role model, in that they have no concept of how to hold a tool, or which tool does what! It may be anecdotal but it may be something you need to consider.

As a teacher other things you may wish to consider include working more closely with parents and carers to involve them in the learning of their 14–19 year old. Most schools and colleges do encourage and establish communication links with families and encourage families to come into the learning place, whether that be for specific events such as parent evenings or for social events.

Within the 14–19 curriculum there are many opportunities for your students to showcase their work, and activities that you may wish to try could be displays, short presentations or fashion shows.

Case study

A large, well-established catering college in the North uses social events to showcase their student learning to wider family networks. Once a year a celebration of achievement event is hosted for families. The menu and theme of the evening is developed by the students, and the meal is cooked and served by the student body. Entertainment is provided by students on media and drama programmes and displays of work from other vocational areas are displayed.

Think about your vocational learners. Is there an opportunity for you to encourage students and families to work more closely with you?

Peer groups

The second area of social learning identified by Cooley is that of peer groups. Peer groups allow individuals to learn how to interact and behave in socially acceptable ways. Group members gain a sense of identity and acquire individual roles and responsibilities within the group. Peer groups can be used to protect young people from being isolated and evidence suggests that young people who are well integrated into a peer group are less likely to withdraw from a programme (Lubell and Vetter, 2006) According to Hargreaves (1967) the influence of peers becomes more important than that of family groups as children move into their teenage years, as the peer group is important in establishing social status and identity.

To encourage and promote peer groups within your classroom there are many strategies that you could use to create both physical and virtual groupings. Small group activities can be used to encourage quieter students to participate and thus build confidence in their own ability. Virtual groups can be set up to have online discussions through blogs, wikis or other asynchronous methods.

Peer learning methods

Peer learning as a term encompasses several teaching and learning practices. 'Peer tutoring', 'peer instruction', 'co-operative or collaborative learning' (group work) and 'peer editing' are just some of the terms referenced in pedagogy discussions. Some practices, such as peer tutoring, fall into the category of peer learning but mostly occur in contexts other than the classroom. Online peer learning can occur through discussion boards, blogs, and wikis rather than face-to-face.

Think-pair-share: After posing a question (particularly a complex one), give students five minutes to think about it, perhaps even to jot down some notes, after which you have them partner up for a quick discussion about what they think and why. After giving ample time for discussion, ask partners to share their insights with the entire class. This is sometimes called 'snowballing' as a teaching and learning strategy. As a technique it provides the students with time to think about the answer to a question or problem and time to discuss it with a cohort, before proposing an answer or solution to the entire class. Regardless of whether the result ends up being shared in the larger class discussion, the process often leads to more thorough, deeper thinking on the part of each student.

Peer tutoring: Give students time in class to pair up in an in-class tutor/tutee relationship – taking turns between being the tutor and the tutee. They will benefit in two ways: 1) from explaining their own personal understanding of the material to another and, 2) from hearing the other explain, from their understanding or viewpoint, the same material.

In this model, students spend time summarising information, assessing the work or ideas of a peer, and explaining rationales that promote critical thinking and long-term retention of information.

Collaborative group work: Many vocational subjects lend themselves to group work and group activities. However, when setting up group tasks you need to have a clear rationale for your groupings. What is the optimum time for the activity? How many will be needed to create the group dynamics? How will you assign group members – randomly or through self-selection? What are the roles within the group? Whilst within your classroom your social peer groups will have identified roles for themselves (class clown, studious one, pragmatist, time-keeper etc), it is interesting to challenge these self- assigned roles through the allocation of specific roles and tasks for a group project.

Activity

Consider a peer group within your 14–19 teaching. How many different roles can you identify within that group? (These may not be directly related to learning, but could be roles such as class clown.)

Assessing peer learning

Formative feedback (non-graded feedback to the learner, designed to modify and improve learning):

- Use verbal feedback during group work. Walk around the room, check in with each group, ask for questions and listen to the group. Group members are more likely to ask more promptly for clarification when you approach them.
- Hold groups accountable by have a quick reporting of groups back to class – either all groups or a random selection. Have note-takers hand in their sheets.
- Respond to group work and involve the class in assessing the benefits of the group's work. Extend the class discussion into new areas and pursue new implications.

Summative feedback ('grades'): Give groups clear information about grading and whether you will use individual or group grades, teacher or peer grades, or some combination.

Community groups

The final group that Cooley (1909) identifies is the community group. These may be special interest groups or vocational groups aligned to the career choice of an individual. The key area here is the development of communities of practice whereby learning happens through social group interaction and situated learning allows the learner to progress through cognitive levels of ability from novice to expert (Lave and Wenger, 1991). The idea of communities of practice (CoP) is that learning occurs in social contexts that emerge and evolve when people who have common goals interact as they strive towards those goals.

Communities of practice

Communities of practice are formed by people who engage in a process of collective learning in a shared domain of human endeavour: a tribe learning to survive, a band of artists seeking new forms of expression, a group of engineers working on similar problems, a clique of pupils defining their identity in the school, a network of surgeons exploring novel techniques, a gathering of first-time managers helping each other cope. In a nutshell: Communities of practice are groups of people who share a concern or a passion for something they do and learn how to do it better as they interact regularly.

(Wenger, circa 2007, based upon Lave and Wenger, 1991)

Within your classroom you have the opportunity to develop communities of practice with your learners. This works well if you have a work-based learning element or are working with apprenticeships, as the community is spread much further than the classroom and encompasses a deeper level of knowledge that comes from the practice and engaging with practitioners. According to Lave and Wenger:

Learners inevitably participate in communities of practitioners and . . . the mastery of knowledge and skill requires newcomers to move toward full participation in the socio-cultural practices of a community. 'Legitimate peripheral participation' provides a way to speak about the relations between newcomers and old-timers, and about activities, identities, artefacts, and communities of knowledge and practice. A person's intentions to learn are engaged and the meaning of learning is configured through the process of becoming a full participant in a socio-cultural practice. This social process includes, indeed it subsumes, the learning of knowledgeable skills.

(Lave and Wenger, 1991: 29)

To take this further Vygotsky (1978) talks about social interaction being an important element for learning. Within communities of practice it is the situation or *situated learning* (Lave and Wenger, 1991) that provides the authenticity of the context in which the learning occurs, thus helping knowledge creation and allowing each individual to apply it in new ways and situations.

Activity

How could you use the concept of situated learning or communities of practice to support your subject area and what learning and teaching activities may be appropriate?

Psychological theories of social learning

The social groups that we belong to can have a profound effect on how we act as individuals and how we perceive ourselves. Teachers have long realised the importance of belonging and group membership and this can be seen in both schools and colleges with the use of houses – the houses of Gryffindor, Hufflepuff, Ravenclaw and Slytherin in the 'Harry Potter' series are a good example of this that most people will recognise. Social learning theories propose that both social life and psychological life interact to form overall learning. As a teacher you can enhance the learning experience by being mindful and aware of the ways in which social and psychological lives can influence your classroom.

Social-emotional development

Social-emotional development provides the foundation for how we feel about ourselves and how we experience others. This foundation begins the day we are born and continues to develop throughout our lifespan. In simple terms emotional development refers to the attainment of emotional capabilities and their expansion as a child grows. These capabilities enable children to have feelings about what they do and about others. Emotional development provides children the capabilities and skills that they need to function and survive in society as well as the world.

Social development is learning the skills that enable a person to interact and communicate with others in a meaningful way. Social skills are closely allied to Emotional Intelligence (EI) – a kind of intelligence or skill that involves the ability to perceive, assess and positively influence one's own and other people's emotions. Some texts include personal skills amongst social and emotional development – in this instance 'personal' is the development of skills related to positive interpersonal relationships within the family, peer groups, workplace, and community.

Personal, social and emotional development is made up of the following aspects:

- Dispositions and attitudes – how children become interested, excited and motivated about their learning.

- Self-confidence and self-esteem – having a sense of their own value, and understanding the need for sensitivity to significant events in their own and other people's lives.

- Making relationships – the importance of forming good relationships with others and working alongside others companionably.

- Behaviour and self-control – how children develop a growing understanding of what is right and wrong and why, together with learning about the impact of their words and actions on themselves and others.

- Self-care – how children gain a sense of self-respect and concern for their own personal hygiene and care and how they develop independence.

- Sense of community – how children understand and respect their own needs, views, cultures and beliefs and those of other people.

Social and emotional development in the 14–19 age phase

As children move through adolescence there are several changes that may manifest in your classroom. Some of these changes may prove to be challenging for you as the teacher and also for the student concerned. This next section considers some of the changes that may be taking place and the implications they could have on learning.

Social changes

Your 14–19 learner could be experiencing many changes within their social development and not all will experience the changes at the same time.

Between the ages of 14–19 young people are often searching for their identity, working out who they are and where they fit in the world. This search can be influenced by gender, peer group, cultural background and family expectations. Within the classroom this may manifest through arguments, heated debate or passion for a particular topic. This can be used to a teaching advantage by making use of group discussion, debate or other activities that harness the learners' passion.

Young people are also seeking more independence, often termed as rebellion, and this could affect how they make decisions (for example, do I do the homework or not?). Hand-in-hand with independence adolescents are looking for more responsibility and new experiences. As a teacher how could you use this to your advantage?

In addition to the above the young learners are starting to question what is right and wrong and you may find them questioning you more in the classroom. Teenagers also learn that they're responsible for their own actions, decisions and consequences, although they are also influenced more by friends, especially when it comes to behaviour, sense of self and self-esteem.

Finally, but by no means least, communication may change in that the 14–19 year old is likely to be more in tune with social media than with you. If that is the case you need to think about how you can use their interest in social media within the classroom. (Chapter 5 gives some ideas of using technology.)

Emotional changes

Teenagers have also been portrayed as showing strong feelings and intense emotions at different times, often with moody and unpredictable outbursts. Remember the Kevin and Perry spoof (Harry Enfield and Kathy Burke) from the early 2000s? These emotions could lead to increased conflict. At the other end of the spectrum, this age group can also be more sensitive to other people's emotions, reading body language and facial expressions.

This age group will also see things differently from you as they begin to think more abstractly and to question different points of view, and often will find it hard to understand the effects of their behaviour and comments on other people.

Theoretical aspects

Whilst not exhaustive the next section will consider some of the approaches and theories underpinning 14–19 learning in the classroom.

Carl Rogers

Carl Rogers is traditionally associated with counselling and psychotherapy. However, he provides some insight and useful advice for learning and teaching activity. Rogers' underlying belief was that most people are able to solve their own problems if provided with a safe environment in which they can explore issues and express themselves openly without fear of retribution. When applied to education, he argues that this philosophy puts the student at the centre of learning, with the teacher acting as the facilitator to provide the environment in which the student can explore and learn. His approach is commonly referred to as student-centred learning.

In simple terms, student-centred learning changes the focus of instruction and places the emphasis on the student with the teacher acting as the facilitator to support and enable learning to happen. Student-centred learning aims to develop learner autonomy and independence by appealing to the social changes that are taking place for the learner. As a concept it encourages problem solving and the need for the student to take responsibility and be active in their own learning.

As a theory, student-centred learning and practice is based on constructivism and relies on students making connections and constructing new knowledge from prior experiences. (See Chapter 5 for more information on constructivism.)

For Carl Rogers one of the keys to student-centred learning, in addition to learning in a secure environment, is the development of a positive self-concept. Self-concept is the view that a person has of themselves as an individual – it may be a positive or negative view. Self-concept arises from an individual's interaction with others through the earlier stages of his or her life. Consider a young adolescent who has been constantly told he will never achieve or go to university. Before long, the self-concept he has becomes a self-fulfilling prophecy and he 'fails'. As a teacher this is an area that you need to be aware of. It often manifests itself as self-esteem, which (although similar to self-concept) is how we feel about ourselves rather than how we view ourselves. For a young person self-concept and self-esteem can go hand-in-hand, or they may contradict each other. For example, you may have a learner who has constantly been told they are excellent, therefore that is their self-concept, yet in reality they are weak and do not get good marks in class and their self-esteem is low.

Case study

Sarah came to you on a Level 2 programme. She has been told she will never achieve, and will end up having three kids before she is 25. As a result Sarah's self-concept is that she is 'thick' and only good for one thing. Her self-esteem is low and she is en-route to a self-fulfilling prophecy. She doesn't take part in class and is out getting drunk every evening. As her teacher you believe that she has the potential to achieve. On the very rare occasions she contributes, she is bright, articulate and has some good ideas and suggestions. How could you encourage Sarah and improve her self-esteem so that she can reach her potential?

The case study above is based upon one of my students. Sarah (not her real name) went onto university and has recently completed her Master's degree. Whilst Sarah was hard work, the dedication and belief that we had in her changed her self-concept to a positive one. As a team we evaluated her preferred learning styles to ensure that we always included content in a way that she found more accessible. We also used peer -mentoring and collaborative group work as a strategy to encourage her to be part of a group where her skills were valued. In this way her contribution and her role in the group started to give her some pride in her ability. Other tactics used were around the types of feedback that we gave. We always ensured that Sarah had at least one positive comment about her input in each session and that in follow up tutorials we used those positives to build upon and provide feed-forward to stretch and challenge her. All Sarah needed was someone who believed in her as her experiences up until arriving at college had all been negative and were creating a self-fulfilling prophecy of failure.

The work of Rosenthal and Jacobsen (1968), among others, shows that teacher expectations influence student performance. Positive expectations influence performance positively, and negative expectations influence performance negatively. Rosenthal and Jacobson originally described the phenomenon as the 'Pygmalion Effect'.

> *When we expect certain behaviors of others, we are likely to act in ways that make the expected behavior more likely to occur.*
>
> *(Rosenthal and Jacobsen, 1968)*

Interventions for social and emotional learning (SEL)

A national programme to target social and emotional learning was introduced in the UK in 2005 to support effective learning, positive behavior, attendance and emotional wellbeing. Three key interventions were identified: programmes taking place within the classroom, specialised targeted programmes, and whole-school approaches designed to support and encourage greater engagement in learning. Evaluation of such programmes indicate that they can have significant impact on attitudes to learning, attainment and social relationships. However, whilst indicating positive outcomes it requires staff to be appropriately trained in interventions.

In England, a number of studies have identified a link between SEL interventions and academic outcomes. However, evidence from the nationwide SEL programme introduced in 2005 does underline the fact that benefits to learning will not be automatically achieved, and that the quality of engagement with the SEL approach is likely to affect outcomes. A quasi-experimental evaluation of the impact of the secondary programme did not find a secure impact on attainment in SEL schools. Similarly, a 2015 randomised controlled trial of an SEL intervention, 'Promoting Alternative Thinking Strategies', found that it did not have a positive impact on academic attainment.

Motivation and self-esteem

As discussed earlier in this chapter, raising self-esteem can have a causal effect and influence on academic attainment. It can itself become a self-fulfilling prophecy in that success can raise self-esteem, which in turn increases success. Therefore as a teacher raising self-esteem is about providing your learner with positive motivation and positive emotional rewards.

One of the most difficult aspects of becoming a teacher is learning how to motivate your students. It is also one of the most important. Students who are not motivated will not learn effectively. They won't retain information, they won't participate and some of them may even become disruptive. A student may be unmotivated for a variety of reasons: they may feel that they have no interest in the subject, find the teacher's methods un-engaging or be distracted by external forces. It may even come to light that a student who appeared unmotivated actually has difficulty learning and is need of special attention.

While motivating students can be a difficult task, the rewards are more than worth it. Motivated students are more excited to learn and participate. Simply put, teaching a class full of motivated students is enjoyable for teacher and student alike. Some students are self-motivated, with a natural love of learning. But even with the students who do not have this natural drive, a great teacher can make learning fun and inspire them to reach their full potential.

Motivation is also an important factor in academic success, and when students are motivated to learn academic achievement can be significantly improved. Motivation can be derived from a number of sources, home, family, recognition, status, or just a sheer passion for the subject area. Motivational theories fall into two

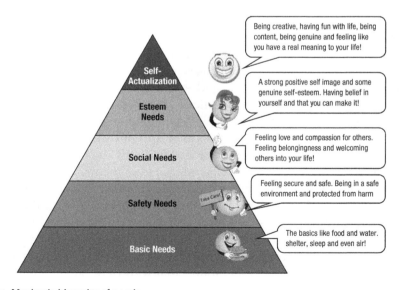

FIGURE 2.1 Maslow's hierachy of needs

main categories: process theories and content theories. The latter is concerned with intrinsic and extrinsic needs, and the former concentrates on cognitive processes.

The most well known of all motivational theories has to be Maslow's Hierachy of Needs, which mirrors some of what we have been discussing in this chapter so far.

Maslow's theory belongs to the process theory family and identifies five basic needs, from the most basic survival needs of food, water, warmth and shelter to what he perceived as being the highest level of motivation, self-actualisation of the individual.

If we take these needs at face value what does it mean for the classroom?

Activity

Consider the five areas Maslow identifies in his hierarchy of needs. What can you do as a teacher to ensure that motivation is at its highest at all times?

You may have considered the environment – is the temperature conducive for learning? Are you providing effective and appropriate feedback and support? Do your students feel valued?

Intrinsic motivation

Intrinsic motivation comes from within the individual. It is driven by curiosity and a desire to learn and find out things. Intrinsic motivation often manifests itself as a hobby in younger adults, a hobby which often stays with them right throughout their adult life.

Extrinsic motivation

Extrinsic motivation comes from outside of the learner. It may be in the form of a reward, or to achieve a goal. It can be quite difficult to manage extrinsic motivation in the classroom if you are dealing with adolescents experiencing the social and emotional changes that can be all encompassing for them. The desire to fit in, look cool and not be 'nerdy' may often win over the intrinsic desire to learn.

If we go back to Maslow we can see how his levels of need can be split into intrinsic and extrinsic factors, the intrinsic being factors internal to the learner (i.e self-esteem) and the extrinsic being those that motivate a response.

Activity

How could you use extrinsic motivation as a learning and teaching method within the classroom?

You may have considered praise or reward as options that are easy to introduce, with very little cost to you as the teacher. Other ways of motivating can be simply praise and encouragement, allowing learners to take control of their learning, and if they have an intrinsic motivation, allowing them to harness it in the classroom. Many teachers don't allow students to wear headphones when doing group work – if music motivates and encourages productivity, why not?

Motivating your learners

To motivate your learners you need to make a positive impression and get them to respect you, whilst at the same time respecting them. Here are a few tips about motivating your 14–19 learner.

Be passionate about what you're teaching. Wide eyes, a grin and barely suppressed enthusiasm does wonders for a student. Even if they're not interested in your subject, your manner would amuse them. Most of all, because you are adamantly expressing your love for a subject, they will tend to mark you as a *genuine* person. My favourite teacher was the history teacher who re-enacted every battle or historical event with rulers and chairs as props!

Be energetic. Enthusiasm is contagious. It is also a lot harder for students to fall asleep in class if the teacher is bouncing off the wall. One of my colleagues is renowned for his enthusiasm for his subject. He always has additional anecdotes, personal stories and additional facts that he peppers his sessions with to make them more interesting.

Appearance. Put an effort into your appearance. You need to make a good impression; make sure you walk into class looking good. You don't want to be mistaken for one of the group. Try to dress a little better or differently than the average person.

Encourage lively class discussion. Don't just talk at your students all the time.

Care. If a learner looks a little down, ask them if they are ok – it shows them that you are interested in them, and if there is a genuine problem it may get them to open up to you.

Attribution theory and self-esteem

Attribution theory is quite simply the idea that an individual attributes their success or failure to something that they can or cannot control. Generally success is attributed to ability which can be controlled and failure is attributed to external factors that cannot be controlled. Students may attribute their inability to grasp a concept to a 'rubbish teacher' or 'when they were talking I couldn't concentrate' rather than their ability to focus or their lack of effort. Within attribution theory people fall into two distinct categories: those with an internal locus of control and those with an external locus of control. The former will be the individuals who are proactive and take pride in achievements whereas the latter avoid responsibility, always blaming others.

Activity

Think about your 14–19 learners. Is it easy to identify into which of the two categories they fall? What could you do transform external loci into internal loci?

Learning and teaching techniques to motivate your 14–19 learner

As we have discussed, the 14–19 learner is undergoing very challenging social and emotional development, which together with his or her self-esteem and motivation could be a concern in the classroom. The following section considers some of the educational implications of the theories that have been examined.

Physiological needs

As we have seen, many of theories discuss the wellbeing and safety of the learner. You may wish to consider some of the following in your classroom:

- Is the room adequately ventilated?
- Is the room an appropriate temperature?
- Does your lesson avoid lengthy periods of passive listening?
- Do you include a range of activities that enable student-centered learning?
- Could you provide any extrinsic rewards? (You would be surprised how motivated even 14/15 year olds can be by stars!)
- Do you have adequate breaks between sessions?
- Do you give appropriate feedback?

Activity

Consider a class of 15-year-old engineers in a Friday afternoon two-hour session straight after lunch in May. What are the likely challenges that you may face in motivating them to learn? What could you do to try and mitigate some of the challenges?

Social needs

If you look back at some of the social and emotional changes that we have discussed in this chapter you could be forgiven for thinking that the 14–19 age group are the most challenging group to teach. As a teacher who started off with 14–19 learners I would agree that there can be challenges, but armed with the correct tool-kit and knowledge they can be overcome, and in my opinion make this age group the most rewarding to work with.

If you consider some of the social elements that are important to an adolescent, there are two main strategies that can be used within your learning and teaching activities. Firstly, you could use small groups for projects or tasks. This will enable you (or the group) to allocate specific tasks, ergo meeting the need to have autonomy and responsibility. Another activity that fits well into small groups is the use of role play. Although not always popular, if used effectively role play can be used to teach some of the skills that are not always well developed in teenagers. For example you could role play an angry customer to introduce problem solving or conflict resolution skills.

The other main strategy is that of using large groups in your learning and teaching. Large groups can create socialisation opportunities and encourage a sense of belonging and identity. Examples of how this can work include study groups, classroom community and whole-group extra-curricular activities (i.e, trips relevant to the subject studied).

Individual needs

We all have individual needs which link to our self-esteem and self-worth. Meeting individual needs is quite often described as ensuring that we use the correct strategies to meet and support individual and specific needs. However, it can be much simpler than that. Knowing and using the names of your learners is the most simple and effective method of promoting a sense of self-worth, followed by listening and acknowledging their contributions in class. Of course, ensuring that students have any specific support is important, but small things can go a long way.

The other areas of need that are important to meet are the cognitive needs of your learners. Is what you are providing relevant? Does it instil confidence in the learners and does it provide them with satisfactory outcomes?

Conclusion

This chapter has explored how a 14–19 learner's mind is working and the social and emotional development stages that he or she will be going through during this stage of adolescence. Whilst it is clear that everyone develops at different rates, having an awareness of some of the impact that these changes could have can help you with your everyday teaching strategies and ensure that you get the best out of your students.

References

Cooley, C.H. (1909) *Social Organisation: A Study of the Larger Mind.* New York: Charles Schribner's Sons.

Hargreaves, D. (1967) *Social Relations in a Secondary School.* London: Routledge and Kegan Paul.

Lave, J. & Wenger, E. (1991) *Situated Learning: Legitimate Peripheral Participation.* Cambridge: Cambridge University Press.

Lubell. K. & Vetter, J. (2006) 'Suicide and youth violence prevention: the promise of an integrated approach', *Aggression and Violent Behaviour,* 11 (2): 167–175.

Rosenthal, R. & Jacobsen, L. (1968) *Pygmalion in the Classroom.* Carmarthen: Crown publishing.

Vygotsky, L. S. (1978) *Mind in Society: The Development of Higher Psychological Processes.* Cambridge, MA: Harvard University Press.

Further reading

This chapter has touched upon some of the social and emotional development needs for your 14–19 learner. To learn more about motivating learners have a look at the following websites for ideas.

www.freeology.com/teacher-humor/40-ways-teachers-motivate-students/

www.teaching.about.com/od/pd/a/Motivate-Students.htm

www.teach.com/what/teachers-change-lives/teachers-motivate

3

Teaching and learning for the 14–19 phase

Learning objectives

After studying this chapter you will be able to:

- provide a brief overview of the range of learning theories;
- discuss a range of learning styles;
- provide definitions for applied and work-related learning;
- discuss the range of learning and teaching methods available for the 14–19 teacher.

Introduction

Everyone learns differently and a 14–19-year-old learner, whether on a vocational programme or a traditional academic programme will have their own preferences for different learning styles and teaching methods. This chapter will review some of the key learning theories and styles that have been used in academic discourse over the last few years that you may find useful in teaching this age phase. Some of you may be familiar with these and just using the chapter as a revision; some of you may be new to teaching and not as familiar with the concepts. Therefore the intention is to provide an overview and recap of some of the main educational theorists together with ideas for using these as a basis in your classroom. Further reading to signpost those of you less experienced within the classroom will be provided at the end of the chapter.

I would start with the suggestion that it is important for any teacher that they have an understanding of some of the theories surrounding teaching and learning in order to be able to make the best choices when planning and delivering classes.

Several schools of learning theory exist that you may wish to draw upon when working with 14–19 students. Indeed it could be argued that 'Perhaps the one certainty about educational ideas is that there can be no consensus' (Halsall and Cockett, 1996: 117).

Let's start by looking at some of the learning theories that you may wish to consider when working with a 14–19 year old student.

Behaviourism

There are a number of prominent theorists who developed the behaviouristic viewpoint: Thorndike, Skinner, Hull and Pavlov to name but a few. Though their ideas vary in detail, they all have some overarching principles in common.

Essentially, behaviourists are interested in overt observable behaviours, rather than internal thoughts such as intentions and wishes. In more detail, they look for the antecedents of behaviour (i.e. what triggers it) and behavioural consequences. Thorndike's (1932) law of effect says that you learn something about your behaviour because of the consequences that it has for you.

Characteristics of behaviorism:

1   Behaviourism is naturalistic. This means that the material world is the ultimate reality, and everything can be explained in terms of natural laws. Man has no soul and no mind, only a brain that responds to external stimuli.

2   A key aspect of behaviourism is that thoughts, feelings, intentions, and mental processes, do not determine what we do. Behaviourism views behaviour as the product of conditioning. Humans are biological machines and do not consciously act; rather they react to stimuli.

3   Consistently, behaviourism teaches that we are not responsible for our actions. If we are mere machines, without minds or souls, reacting to stimuli and operating on our environment to attain certain ends, then anything we do is inevitable.

4   Behaviourism is manipulative. It seeks not merely to understand human behaviour, but to predict and control it.

The main concept underpinning behaviourist learning theories is that the learner responds to a stimuli in a stimulus/response relationship. As a concept, behaviourism originated with the work of John B. Watson, an American psychologist whose work was based on the experiments of Ivan Pavlov. These experiments, commonly called Pavlov's dogs, observed the responses that dogs had to the use of a bell at feeding time. The eventual behaviour observed over time was that just the use of the bell could create the response, in this case salivation.

In 1938 Skinner took these principles further and suggested that if an environment was structured in a manner that enables positive outcomes, then through a method of conditioning outcomes would always be positive.

From his theories, Skinner developed the idea of 'shaping'. By controlling rewards and punishments, you can shape the behaviour of another person.

LOUD BELL   ⟹   JUMP

Over time the stimulus can be linked to new forms of behaviour for example:

LOUD BELL   ⟹   LUNCH BREAK/FOOD

This then becomes a learnt behaviour, and a loud bell is associated with eating, so you feel hungry. The learners are therefore conditioned to respond in a particular way. I use this as concept in my classes to bring learners back together again following a group or individual task. For example, a simple switching on or off of the lights signals that I wish the group to be quiet; other noises and gestures signal other behaviours. A particular favourite with younger learners is the croaking frog. This is a signal that the time allocated for the group task has expired and we need regroup and discuss. The frog itself is a simple wooden frog that allows you to create a croaking noise buy running a wooden stick across the frog's back. Simple, but effective and just one of a myriad of props that you could have in your repertoire.

If we relate the theory of behaviourism to the wider remit of vocational learning we could perhaps suggest that using teacher demonstration followed by a student copying and repeating a particular work-based skill would be an appropriate method to use within the classroom, as skills cannot be acquired without practice and the opportunity to 'get it wrong' in a safe environment. What is clear is that as a theory behaviourist learning is an obvious choice. For example, if we look at early child education, whereby rewards can be given for appropriate behaviour, and punishment for inappropriate behaviour, we are clearly using Skinner's positive and negative reinforcement strategies. It is also true to say that the act of repetition and active learning or 'learning by doing' is more effective than passive learning.

However, as teachers do we need to consider how we test a learner's understanding of a particular skill if they have been taught through a purely behaviourist approach and conditioned to respond in a certain way? Consider the following: how could you ensure that your learners could explain as well as do a particular task?

Case study

Paul assesses electrical installation students. He is frustrated that during his assessment of learners, the learners can quite often complete the task required of them, but are then not able to explain their actions, nor repeat them if slight changes are made to the assessment set up. He believes that they have been taught using a behaviourist approach.

How appropriate is this if the skills are supposed to be work-related and, more importantly, transferable to the work place?

Behaviourist approaches have proved to be extremely valuable in education and training over the last few years and many teachers still use them in the classroom today.

Activity

As part of your own professional development, observe a more experienced member of your team with your 14–19 learners. What aspects of behaviourism theory can you see being used in the session? How could you adopt or adapt it for your own use?

Constructivism

Constructivism as a paradigm posits that learning is an active process and that learners construct their own knowledge. As a theory, constructivism is based on observation and scientific study about how people learn. It argues that people construct their own understanding and knowledge of the world, through experiencing things and reflecting on their own personal experiences. When we encounter something new, we have to reconcile it with our previous ideas and experience, maybe changing what we believe, or maybe discarding the new information as irrelevant. In essence, constructivist theory believes that we create our own knowledge by asking questions, exploring ideas and assessing what we already know.

Kolb's four part cyclical learning cycle demonstrates this in more detail.

In the classroom, the constructivist view of learning can point towards a number of different teaching practices. Commonly, constructivist techniques are active techniques, or experiential learning, such as experiments or real-world problem solving. These techniques create knowledge which can then be reflected upon. Constructivism transforms the student from a passive recipient of information to an active participant in the learning process. Always guided by the teacher, students construct their knowledge actively rather than just mechanically ingesting knowledge from the teacher or the textbook.

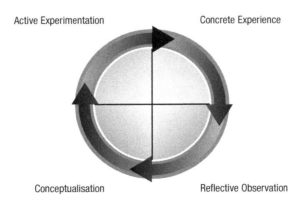

FIGURE 3.1 Kolb's learning cycle

Adapted from Senior, 2010

If we consider our vocational 14–19 learner, how can we best make use of this theory in our planning? One of the most effective ways to allow your learner to explore his or her knowledge and to build upon it is to use the concept map, developed from the original 'schema theory' put forward by Piaget (1896–1980). Piaget believed that when you encounter something new you either assimilate it into what you know already, or you have to accommodate it by creating new sets of information, like opening a new file when you start a new subject. For example, Psychology is a bit like Sociology, so you will group the two until you know more about one or other. This new subject then needs its own set of information. The original theory suggested that human beings create mental maps to allow them to understand what was happening around them. For our 14–19 learners the use of the concept map can aid learning by allowing them to discover and make connections between any two points. Figure 3.2 shows a concept map that represents the impacts of mass tourism on a small fishing village.

Although this example is incomplete and many more strands could be added to extend the information, as a strategy the method can be used as an initial tool to create discussion amongst learners. It can also allow you to assess prior knowledge if done as a starter activity, provide you with an overview of their understanding of the topic if used as a plenary activity, and if used within the main body of the session it can be used as a collaborative learning tool to allow students to share ideas and add or build upon their original thoughts. Colour can be introduced to demonstrate different key points (e.g. the positive and negative effects or the different types of effect that the village may experience). If used throughout a programme of learning students can add to it as their knowledge develops, making different connections and adding different areas for discussion.

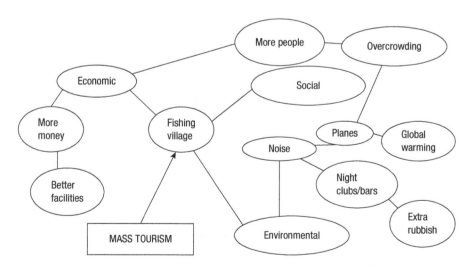

FIGURE 3.2 Impacts of mass tourism on a small fishing village

(Senior, 2010)

As a theory of how people learn, this theory, coupled with Kolb's learning cycle, would imply that your students will try something (useful for practical work-related skills), reflect upon how it went, make mental adjustments and retry. For example, a student could build a brick wall, reflect upon how they laid and sorted the bricks, decide whether the process undertaken was the best way or whether there were any other better ways of laying the bricks, and next time use the new idea.

As a teacher you will need to consider this cycle when teaching work-related or practical skills and assess how and if the learners progress around the framework and the steps you can take to reduce frustration and improve the learning experience for all.

Other theorists that you may wish to explore within the field of constructivism are Bruner (1915–) who believes that learning is a social process in which learners construct understanding through interaction and communication. As a learning theory Bruner's theory has three main elements: the acquisition of knowledge, the transformation of knowledge and the evaluation of knowledge. He advocates the use of discovery learning as the most effective method for problem solving. As a method it is based on student-centred approaches in which the role of the teacher is to provide opportunities for learning. In other words, 'teaching by asking' rather than 'teaching by telling' (Petty, 2004).

Vygotsky (1896–1934) is a further constructivist theorist worth mentioning here, as his work revolved around challenging learners to achieve by providing scaffolding to help them to progress. This allows the learner to achieve in a secure and safe environment, but only if the teacher knows the learner and his or her ability. This is where the use of individual learning plans and the initial advice and guidance plays a crucial part in your classroom activities.

Humanism

As a learning theory, the humanistic approach removes all barriers to learning and replaces them with positive thoughts and experiences. In essence the humanistic approach creates a safe environment for the learner to learn in, based on:

- warmth (you feel welcome);
- genuiness (people are honest and friendly with you);
- unconditional positive regard (they will like you no matter how you behave).

This builds positive self-esteem, confidence and a willingness to try new things, where students help to drive the learning process, and can follow areas of interest.

Humanistic educators believe that both feelings and knowledge are important to the learning process. Unlike traditional educators, humanistic teachers do not separate the cognitive and affective domains. This aspect also relates to the curriculum in the sense that lessons and activities provide focus on various aspects of the student and not just rote memorisation through note-taking and lecturing.

Activity

Consider your teaching sessions. How do you create a safe and supportive learning environment for your students? What humanistic approaches have you used, or could you use to encourage the less motivated students to engage?

Learning styles

The term 'learning style' is an umbrella term used within educational circles that covers a range of different ways in which people learn, or their preferred way of learning. If you think back to your school days, how did your teachers teach you? If I think about my school years 11–18, I seem to remember being told things and having to write it down. There was very little opportunity for me to 'have a go' at something or even watch a video about something. The nearest we got to video was a history teacher re-enacting the Battle of Agincourt with a ruler! I do not recall any group work, any activities or any opportunity for me to problem-solve. Consequently, at times we were unruly and disruptive as our needs as learners were not being met. One of my favourite memories was spending an entire lesson sitting under the desk playing cards, while the teacher in charge never noticed, just continued dictating! So, knowing a little about learning styles and preferred learning styles may if nothing else save you from the 15-year-old-poker players.

A recent survey by Coffield, Mosely, Hall and Ecclestone (2004) suggested that there were over 70 different learning styles systems. However, most teacher training and continuing professional development (CPD) programmes tend to concentrate on a favoured few: Kolb, VAK, Honey and Mumford, and Gardiner's multiple intelligences. Let's explore these and identify whether they are useful for the 14–19 learner.

Honey and Mumford

Honey and Mumford (1986) take Kolb's learning cycle a little further and suggest that each stage within the cycle can be defined as a preferred learning style. They suggest that there are four different learning styles, each having its own characteristics and preferences when it comes to the classroom. The four styles are:

- Activists
- Reflectors
- Theorists
- Pragmatists

For you as the teacher, identifying the type of learner that you are dealing with may help you plan more effectively and include relevant activities within your

TABLE 3.1 Preferred behaviours of different learning types

Preferred	Non-preferred
Activists	
Working in groups	Listening for long periods
Taking the lead in discussions	Note-taking
New and challenging experiences	Following instructions
	Working alone
Reflectors	
Observing	Short lead-in time
Reflecting and thinking about tasks	Being put on the spot
	Deadlines on activities
Theorists	
Questioning	Unclear instructions
Structure and logical progression	Lack of structure to sessions
A purpose	
Pragmatists	
Links to theory and practice	No perceived benefit to the learning
Examples of good practice	
Guidelines	
Purpose to learning	

(Senior, 2010)

classes. The following table, adapted from Scales (2008), highlights some of the likes and dislikes of these four different learner types.

Gardiner's multiple intelligences

Gardiner's multiple intelligences theory (1993) was developed out of a concern that most intelligence was measured on linguistic or mathematical capabilities. Gardiner suggested that these two narrow definitions prevented some people from demonstrating things that they were good (or intelligent) at. Each of Gardiner's intelligence types is linked to personal characteristics or preferred methods of learning. Again, as with most learning theories, we need to be a little cautious as our learners may display a mixture of one or more of these intelligence types. However, it is a useful tool for any teacher who is struggling to get a particular idea or concept through to a group. Whilst working with a group of 16-year-old learners in a school, one of the group members was really struggling

TABLE 3.2 Gardiner's multiple intelligences

Intelligence	Learning preference
Linguistic	Language, words, writing, speaking and listening
Mathematical	Patterns, problems, logic
Visual	Use of mental images and visual aids
Interpersonal	Like working with others
Intrapersonal	Reflective learners
Bodily	Movement
Musical	Rhythm, pitch
Naturalistic	Observing nature and environment

to understand a particular tourism concept. As the teacher, I had tried verbal explanation, visual explanation and collaborative practices, in the hope one of his peers could help him see the light, all to no avail. It was only when the class decided to create a rap song for part of their assessment that my learner had his 'eureka' moment. This learner is an example of someone with musical intelligence, as defined by Gardiner. Further attempts at engaging this particular student worked really well if music or chant (rhythm) was introduced.

Gardner said that multiple intelligences were not limited to the original eight, and he has since considered the existence and definitions of other possible intelligences in his later work (for example, spiritual/existential and moral). However, these intelligences are difficult to define and, not surprisingly, there have been many debates and interpretations of these potential additions to the model. It is for this reason that you will probably only come across the eight listed above.

Activity

Consider each of Gardiner's intelligences. How might you cater for them in your classroom? Identify one activity for each type

---

Visual Audio Kinaesthetic (VAK)

VAK as a learning style theory categorises learners into three distinct types, and is probably one of the most simplistic learning styles to use. Although recent research would argue that VAK is not scientific and doesn't exist, I am, for the purposes of exploring potential learning styles, including it here for you to make your own decision as to whether it is a useful theory to draw upon.

It suggests that the visual learner likes to see and use pictures and diagrams to help them learn, such as pictures on PowerPoint slides or diagrams on the board. The audio learner likes to listen, either to the teacher or other auditory input, and the kinaesthetic learner likes to be doing, to be moving and to generally being active in a class.

Many learners will have a preference but it is probably true to say that most learners will be a mixture of the three, depending upon the topic being discussed.

Activity

Consider your last session. What did you do to cater for the three different learning styles discussed above? Could you have done anything any different? Do you believe that making changes may have improved outcomes?

Teaching and learning methods for 14–19 vocational learners

Vocational pedagogy

Pedagogy as a term refers to the science, art, and craft of teaching. Pedagogy also fundamentally includes the decisions which are taken in the creation of the broader learning culture in which teaching takes place, and the values which inform all interactions. The last two to three years have seen a growing interest in vocational pedagogy and the debate as to whether it should be different to what we traditionally class as pedagogy. The Commission on Adult Vocational Education explored and reviewed the quality, outcomes and impact of adult vocational teaching and learning with a view to developing a framework of pedagogical approaches. The initial response to this review can be found here: http://repository.excellence-gateway.org.uk/fedora/objects/eg:6878/datastreams/DOC/content (accessed 15 November 2015).

Regardless of whether there is a need for a specific vocational pedagogical framework, what is known is that vocational education and the 14–19 sector is unique and challenging in that it sits within the duality of traditional educational places (i.e. schools and colleges and the workplace), with some arguing that the skills and expertise of the practitioners involved are different and need to be different to deal with the diverse needs of the learners involved.

What is required in vocational education is that the learners achieve the following:

- Routine expertise: mastery of everyday working procedures.
- Resourcefulness: having the knowledge and aptitude to stop and think effectively when required.
- Functional literacies.
- Craftsmanship: an attitude of pride and thoughtfulness towards the job.

- Business-like attitudes: understanding the economic and social sides of work.
- Wider skills for growth.

Adapted from www.skillsdevelopment.org

In practice, this means that as practitioners we need to ensure that our learners have the necessary skills and expertise to be able to perform tasks effectively, whether that be change a plug, book a holiday or colour someone's hair. They also require what are sometimes referred to as soft skills, the personal, thinking and learning skills (e.g. the ability to be able to work alone and make decisions). So if we consider the theories discussed in the first part of this chapter, what practically can we do to provide our learners with these abilities?

The Centre for Real World Learning produced a framework that provides us with some suggestions of the types of activity that we could use (see Activity below).

Activity

Visit the web page **www.tinyurl.com/j8a724j**
How could you adapt this in your teaching for vocational learners?

For me, the main purpose of vocational education is to provide the learner with the skills and competencies required to work in a particular vocational setting. It follows therefore that what we are teaching and ultimately assessing is their ability to complete tasks effectively, whether in a workplace setting or a work-related environment. This for me makes vocational education different to traditional academic education, as if we choose to assess through written work how can we assess competency?

Therefore, in order to be an effective teacher of vocational education there needs to be a wide range of teaching and learning methods to meet the demands of a wide range of learners across a variety of skills and competencies. As we have already seen, we can base our choice of methods upon learning theories and the learning styles of our students. However, as a teacher we need to ensure that whatever methods we choose to employ in our classroom are methods that we are comfortable with and methods that suit our subject area. Consider the electrician who relies on PowerPoint presentations to demonstrate the correct way to wire a three pin plug. I am sure that there are other, more appropriate methods that could be used for this type of activity.

The following list is by no means exhaustive, but considers some of the techniques that can be used to incorporate work-related and applied learning into your classroom delivery.

- Demonstration
- Role play
- Concept mapping

- Discovery learning
- Problem-based learning
- Projects
- Presentations and market place activities (collaborative learning)

Some of these techniques are detailed below.

Demonstrations

As a teaching activity a demonstration is a good way in which to show your learners a particular skill. In essence a demonstration is about showing another person how to do something.

Quite often teachers shy away from demonstrations because of the practical nature of them and the need to ensure that you have all of the relevant materials to complete the demonstration.

Role play

As a technique, role play can be very useful when used correctly, and more importantly if you have the learners who are comfortable with role playing. Some learners may find the whole concept embarrassing and refuse to take part, whilst others may love being the centre of attention and be the constant volunteer. Think back to the section on humanistic approaches to learning – for many of your learners the role play may not feel safe. However, it can have its advantages in that it allows you to simulate 'real life' situations without the risks that may be associated with the situation.

Projects

A project can have many different connotations, dependent upon the subject area involved. It could take the form of a written report on a particular aspect of a subject, or it could be more practical, such as a video looking at a particular aspect of the subject.

Planning for learning

It has often been said that 'if you fail to plan you plan to fail'. Systematic planning is crucial in all areas of education, not just the 14–19 phase, and is needed to ensure that the delivered curriculum meets both the needs of the learner, and in the case of vocational education, the workplace and employer. According to Fawbert (2008) planning is the bridge between you identifying the needs of your learners and the learning activities that you need to include to meet those needs.

The scheme of work is the first important step to take to effectively manage your planning. A scheme of work is an overview of your proposed delivery and content. They are working documents and should be reviewed regularly to ensure that your learners are monitoring progress against the course outcomes. A scheme of work is usually drawn up based upon the content of the syllabus or module. The key component parts to consider when starting to devise your scheme of work are the following:

- Aims of the programme
- Learning outcomes
- Content
- Teaching and learning strategies
- Assessment strategies
- Course evaluation

The scheme of work should identify the topics that you need to cover to meet the aims of the programme and the learning outcomes, and should consider a logical sequence of events, taking into account any special requirements such as computer labs, field work, etc.

When I write schemes of work I find it easier to use a mind map to identify the topics that I need to cover and the links between them, and therefore the sequencing of each event.

Case study

Cheryl is a trainee teacher at a local FE college. She has been asked to draw up a scheme of work for the following unit of a Level 2 technical certificate in tourism.
The learner can:

1   identify different **types of tourists and groups of tourists**, which travel to UK tourism destinations
2   identify the specific **appeal** of tourism destinations
3   identify **sources** of information about tourism destinations
4   describe the **facilities and services** which may be required by different types of tourists
5   describe **types of accommodation** and **classifications** available at tourism destinations
6   describe types of **catering facilities** available at tourism destinations.

To create the scheme of work she chose to use a mind map to create topic areas, content and sequencing.
What key themes would you suggest were appropriate?
Produce a mind map for teaching this unit

Lesson planning

A lesson plan can be described as a road map that provides the structure for a lesson. Although in recent times they have become a requirement of inspections, both internal and external, a lesson plan should never be so rigid that you cannot deviate from it if you feel there is a need to. Many beginning teachers are so concerned about covering everything they have in their plan and sticking to the timings that they often miss opportunities to enhance learning by allowing extra discussion time or questions.

All lessons should be creative. This is even more important with vocational education as you need to connect the learning to real- life situations. A lesson should emphasise the application of theory to practice through interactive and thought-provoking activity. The key features of a creative lesson plan will provide opportunities for students to ask questions, interact with each other and enable them to take control over their learning. In a creative lesson the teacher becomes more of a facilitator, enabling student-centred learning.

Research exists that suggests that clear starting and ending activities can help to shape learning. Whilst a lesson is part of an holistic overview within the scheme of work, each lesson is a unique moment in time and should be classed as discrete. Therefore as a teacher you should consider the aim of each lesson and what you require the learning outcomes to be. I would always advocate sharing the outcomes with your learners at the start of the session and returning to them at the end to assess whether they have been achieved. The starter activity should then include the sharing of objectives, assessment of prior knowledge and any links from previous sessions. Conversely, the end of the session should check student knowledge, revisit the objectives and make links to future sessions.

When thinking about individual lessons there are four important factors to consider:

- Who are your learners?
- What are the requirements of the course?
- What content should be covered?
- What resources and teaching methods should you use?

The table below provides an example of a lesson plan, aimed to introduce trainee teachers to curriculum theory.

From this example you can see that a lesson plan has clear objectives that you wish to achieve at the end of the session, together with a range of activities that will enable you to meet those objectives.

Writing good lesson objectives can help you plan effectively and motivate and engage your learners on the topic. When writing lesson objectives there are two acronyms that are commonly used for planning purposes: SMART and RUMBA.

SMART stands for specific, measurable, achievable, relevant and timed.

RUMBA stands for relevant, understandable, measurable, behavioural and achievable.

TABLE 3.3 Example lesson plan

AIM: Introduce students to different curriculum models and their appropriateness to post-14 education.

OBJECTIVES:

- Discuss the main traditions of curriculum theory.
- Evaluate the two main curriculum models and their role in post-14 education.
- Discuss curriculum design models and identify the most appropriate for their personal teaching roles.

RESOURCES:

Flip chart

White board

Data projector/laptop

DIFFERENTIATION:

- Different activities to suit different learning styles

REFLECTION/EVALUATION

TIME	TOPIC	ACTIVITY	RESOURCE
1300–1315	Introduction to session, aims and objectives	Didactic link back to last week	PowerPoint
1315–1345		Students Q&A and discussion in relation to their teaching	MindGenius
1345–1415	Mind map traditions of curriculum theory		Board – Pyramid
1415–1445		PowerPoint Q&A	
1445–1455	Curriculum models –product	Student group work and feedback	
1455–1500	Advantages and disadvantgages of product model	Student task and didactic	
	Process model – theory	Didactic and Q&A	
	Teacher v facilitator	Discussion	
	Pedagogy v andragogy debate	Group work and feedback	
	Their role	Individual evaluation	
	Course design models	MindGenius and Q&A	
	Evaluation of own curriculum	Paired discussion	
	Recap objectives and learning		

Activity

Look at the lesson plan above. Are the objectives SMART or RUMBA objectives? Would you re-write them? If so what changes would you make?

Conclusion

In general terms, planning teaching sessions can be seen to be relatively straight-forward and uncomplicated. However, as this chapter has suggested, the teacher needs to take into account many different and competing theories of how people learn to produce lessons that are exciting, motivating and engaging for all. There are several theories of learning that you may wish to consider when planning your curriculum and writing schemes of work that meet the outcome for the programme.

As a process, teaching and learning is not predictable and a teacher needs to be pre-pared to deviate from what is planned and respond to what is happening in the class-room at any given point in time. One of the most important skills to learn as a teacher, whether a beginning teacher or someone who has more experience, is the skill of being able to read our learners and how they are receiving the materials being provided and the ways in which the lesson is being presented. Schemes of work and lesson plans should not be rigid documents and should be used as a framework to develop learn-ing and motivate our students. Vocational pedagogy as a framework also requires us to be cognisant of the real-world environment that our learners are working within, and our planning needs to ensure that learning is relevant for the subject in question, whether through work-placement, work-related learning or work-based learning.

References

Coffield, F., Mosely, D., Hall, E. & Ecclestone, K.(2004), *Should we Be Using Learning Styles?* London: Learning and Skills Research Centre.

Fawbert, F. (2008) *Teaching in Post-Compulsory Education* (2nd Edition). London: Continuum.

Gardiner, G. (1993) *Multiple Intelligences: New Horizons*. New York: Basic Books.

Halsall, R., & Cockett, M., (1996), *Education and Training 14–19: Chaos or Coherence?* London: David Fulton.

Honey, P. & Mumford, A. (1986) *The Manual of Learning Styles*. Maidenhead, Peter Honey.

Petty, G. (2004) *Teaching Today* (3rd edition). Cheltenham: Nelson Thornes.

Scales, P. (2008) *Teaching in the Lifelong Learning Sector*. London: Open University Press.

Senior, L. (2010) *The Essential Guide to Teaching 14–19 Diplomas*. London: Pearson.

Thorndike E. L. (1932) *The Fundamentals of Learning*. New York: Teachers College, Columbia University.

Further reading

DCSF (2004) *Work-related Learning and the Law*. Nottingham: DCSF.

DfE (2015) *Post-16 Work Experience as a Part of 16 to 19 Study Programmes and Traineeships Departmental Advice for Post-16 Education and Training Providers*. London: DfE.

Ginnis, P. (2002), *The Teacher's Toolkit,* Carmarthen: Crown House Publishing.

Johns, A., Miller, A. & the Centre for Education and Industry (2002) *Work Experience and the Law: The Essential Guide for Central Organisers, Employers, Schools and Colleges* (www.backingyoungsuffolk.files.wordpress.com/2011/05/work_experienceandthe_law-v3.pdf).

Scales, P. (2013), *Teaching in the Lifelong Learning Sector,* Maidenhead: Open University Press.

www.crb.gov.uk

www.doceo.co.uk

www.hse.gov.uk/legislation/hswa.htm

www.nebpn.org/cgi-bin/WEX_casestudysectorsearch.cgi (The National Education Business Partnership Network [NEBPN]).

www.qca.org.uk/14-19/11-16-schools/index_s7-0-case-studies.htm (Qualifications and Curriculum Authority).

www.safelearner.info

www.ssatrust.org.uk/vocationallearning/workrelatedlearning/casestudies/default.aspa (Specialist Schools and Academies Trust).

www.teachernet.gov.uk/

Assessing learning in the 14–19 sector

Introduction

Having discussed some of the ways in which you can bring your classroom alive and incorporate an element of applied and work-related learning in the previous chapter, we now need to consider how we assess the 14–19 learner and their learning.

This chapter explores assessment in general terms and focuses on assessment principles and strategies that can be used in the 14–19 phase.

Concepts and principles of assessment

It is almost impossible to describe curriculum and assessment separately: since the late 1970s they have been inextricably linked.

(Haywood, 2007: 254)

Before we start to look at assessment in any great detail we need to understand what is meant by assessment and why we as teachers need to assess our learners.

Within the world of education, and vocational education in particular, assessment is often equated to testing. Often this 'testing' is undertaken to assess whether a student can perform a specific task or skill. With vocational education this testing can take place either within the workplace or more commonly within an education work-related environment that has been set up as a simulation.

Activity: testing in practice

Robert works at a local further education college teaching electrical installation to a range of 14–19 learners. Some learners are on day-release from their employer, some are on an apprenticeship pathway and some are studying full time. All learners are required to demonstrate competency in fault-finding on electrical circuits. In order to assess this skill Robert has built dummy rooms within one of the electrical workshops and is able to put faults into the wiring circuit for students to find. All of his learners are assessed in the same way.

Is this an appropriate way of assessing?

Could he assess his day-release or apprentices in the workplace? What would be the advantages and disadvantages of both approaches?

However, despite the perception of an assessment as being a test, as a teacher we should be using assessment for much more than testing. As a concept, assessment can serve a variety of functions and have several meanings depending upon whether we are the teacher or the learner. For the teacher, assessment can provide an overview of a student's progress, measure the distance travelled, identify any problems that the learner may have with a particular skill or area of knowledge, determine any issues that there may be with the curriculum and help us to evaluate how effective our teaching and the course has been. For the learner it can be a double-edged sword. It can inspire, motivate and provide them with long-term goals and the determination to succeed in their chosen career path. However, it could also have the opposite effect if the learner perceives and equates assessment with testing and feels that the assessment was a negative experience, and that they are failing or not doing as well as they thought.

So why do we even bother with assessment and assessing learners if it can have such potential negative consequences? Talent, excellence and flair do need to be recognised, but this must not de-motivate weaker students. Let's put this into context with the driving test – a test that most of us will recognise, even if we have not had the pleasure of sitting it. The normal pass rate indicates that that 30–40% of learners fail first time around, but the eventual pass rate is 95% of all learners. What we need to remember when assessing our learners is that intelligence, aptitude or ability are measures of *how quickly* students can learn, not, as is often assumed, a measure of *what* they can learn.

For all teachers, regardless of the sector in which they are working, assessment or testing, will be an unavoidable part of the teaching role. Further to the reasons mentioned in the previous paragraph (measuring progress, identifying issues, motivating, inspiring and challenging), what we must remember is that most of the teaching and learning that takes place within the UK educational system is linked to the requirements of an external awarding body or examination board. These are the organisations that provide the proof, or certification, that the learner has reached the required level of knowledge and understanding of the qualification specification. In addition to this, as they provide the overall certification upon completion of a programme of study, we as teachers are required to measure and test our learners against the standards of performance that they have identified within the qualification specification. It is our role to provide the proof that the learners have reached the standards set down by these external agencies.

Moreover, measuring our learners against the external agency standards also provides both us and the external bodies a measure of standardisation across the UK, as all learners will be measured against the same outcomes. Failure to achieve these external standards could result in loss of funding to our institutions and in some cases we could risk our provision being closed down. Therefore, as a note of caution, we as teachers need to be careful that our assessments are not assessments for assessment's sake and that we are providing a broader learning experience, not teaching only what the student needs to pass.

Assessment practices can fall into four broad categories: initial assessment, formative assessment, summative assessment and ipsative assessment.

Initial assessment

Initial assessment, also called diagnostic assessment, is the assessment that would normally take place at the start of a programme or course. It is used primarily to assess student needs and their starting levels prior to enrolment. Initial (diagnostic) assessment involves the gathering and careful evaluation of detailed data using students' knowledge and skills in a given learning area. The data assist teachers to plan for appropriate pedagogy and targeted learning to more effectively scaffold the learning needs of their students. Many schools and colleges have pre-set diagnostic tests for their learners which help to identify any learning disabilities (e.g. dyslexia). However, as a teacher you can also make use of diagnostic assessment in your lesson starter to assess prior learning of a topic or subject area.

Initial assessment techniques

The following list gives some suggestions of initial assessment activities that you could use in the class.

- Quiz – quizzes are a good way of introducing a topic to a group of learners and assessing their prior knowledge. You can also return to the quiz towards the end of the topic to assess what learning has taken place.

- Mind map – asking learners to create a visual map of what they know about a topic will enable you as the teacher to identify where the group have strengths and which areas will need further development. Mind maps can also be used throughout the topic and learners can add to them as they gain more knowledge.

- Grafitti wall – a similar idea to the mind map, but learners are asked to write ideas and thoughts on flip chart paper, or, if you are lucky enough, on the writing wall. Learners can also use post-its rather than writing directly onto the wall. Again, this allows the teacher to gauge the prior knowledge and areas that are weaker.

Formative assessment

Formative assessment takes place during the learning. It is an ongoing process that checks progress and supports further development. Formative assessment can also be called assessment for learning.

Assessment for learning (AFL)

Assessment for learning focuses on the learning process and is conducted during daily sessions. This approach allows students to work with teachers to identify learning objectives and enables feedback to improve the learning. In classes where assessment for learning takes place, the student is encouraged to be more active and participative in their learning and associated assessment. The ultimate purpose of assessment for learning is to create self-regulated learners who can leave education able and confident to continue learning throughout their lives. As a teacher we need to know where our students are in terms of their learning and then continually check on how they are progressing. The teacher and student work together to assess the student's knowledge, what she or he needs to learn to improve and extend this knowledge, and how the student can best get to that point (formative assessment). Assessment for learning occurs at all stages of the learning process.

AFL and formative assessment techniques

Formative assessment is one of the easiest types of assessment to do as it should take place naturally within the classroom. Although not an exhaustive list, the following gives some ideas that you can use:

- Observations can help teachers determine what students do and do not know. There are several instruments and techniques that teachers can use to record useful data about student learning – short notes and student cards to name but a few.
- Questioning – asking better questions affords students an opportunity for deeper thinking and provides teachers with significant insight into the degree and depth of student understanding. Questions of this nature engage students in classroom dialogue that expands student learning. Questions should go beyond the typical factual questions requiring recall of facts or numbers.

- Quizzes can be used during the formative assessment process to monitor student learning and adjust instruction during a lesson or unit. Constructive quizzes will not only furnish teachers with feedback on their students, but also serve to help students evaluate their own learning.

- Individual whiteboards are a great way to hold all students in the class accountable for their work. They actively involve students in the learning and are a terrific tool in the formative assessment process because they give the teacher immediate information about student learning. When students complete their work and hold their whiteboard up, the teacher can quickly determine who is understanding and who needs help, and adjust his or her instruction accordingly.

- Interactive voting – similar to whiteboards and quizzes, interactive voting apps allow students to choose what they believe to be an appropriate answer to a question and for the teacher to assess class or individual progress.

Activity

Before looking at summative and ipsative assessment techniques, think about how you use assessment for learning with your students. Are there other ways in which you could use formative assessment more effectively?

Summative assessment

Summative assessment normally takes place at the end of a programme of study or unit, and is the final measure of the outcome of the programme. It often culminates in a grade, as with GCSE or A-level qualifications, but quite often with vocational education it can just be a measure of competency. Summative assessment results are often benchmarked against other providers.

Types of summative assessment

End-of-unit tests, final exams, mid-term exams and quarterly tests are considered summative assessments. However, not all units and programmes have exams and as a teacher you have the option to decide what your summative assessment will be. Summative assessments can take many forms, including multiple-choice, true-or-false, concept vocabulary matching, fill-in-the-blank and short-answer question tests, presentations, written reports or essays. One summative assessment may contain a combination of these types of questions or can be comprised exclusively of one type of question. It is also important to note that there may be an externally set summative assessment for the programme or programmes that you are teaching. Normally, externally set assessment is also marked externally and provides the awarding bodies with an overview of progress across a range of areas (e.g. male/female variances, regional variances, to name but a few). This data can then be used to set standards or benchmarks for programmes, which all organisations can measure against.

Summative assessment results are often recorded as scores or grades that are then factored into a student's permanent academic record, whether they end up as letter grades on a report card or test scores used in the college admissions process. While summative assessments are typically a major component of the grading process in most schools, colleges and courses, not all assessments considered to be summative are graded.

Ipsative assessment

Ipsative assessment is a type of self-assessment that enables learners to measure their own progress without comparing themselves to their peers or any external benchmarks. As a technique, ipsative assessment works best when it is used in conjunction with initial assessment and individual learning plans. For example, your learners can produce an action plan with targets that they can use to assess progress. For your learners, a good action plan that demonstrates progress can be a powerful tool to increase their self-confidence and self-esteem.

Norm-referencing and criterion referencing

When discussing forms of assessment, the word referencing (as in norm-referencing or criterion referencing) refers to what the learner is compared to, or what the benchmark is for the learner. In ipsative assessment the learner is compared against their own previous performances.

Norm-referencing is more commonly associated with summative assessment, whereby the assessment is a formal, externally marked piece of work where judgements about an individual's performance is compared against another group of learners. Norm-referencing is based on the concept that in any group of learners there will be those who are very able and get the highest grades, some who are not able and fail, and a range in the middle. Within a norm-referencing system grades and grade boundaries are set against these notions and roughly the same number of students are consistently allocated against the grades each time that assessment takes place.

As a system, norm-referencing remains popular with external bodies, such as the government and awarding bodies, as it enables them to produce statistical information and league table data sets.

At the opposite end of the scale, criterion referenced learners are assessed against pre-determined standards without any comparison to their peers. Criterion referencing is based upon the skills, knowledge and understanding that are required for a particular subject or vocation.

Competence-based assessment

Competence-based assessment is a more specialised, vocationally situated assessment that is based upon criterion referencing. Competence-based assessment uses a system whereby each vocational area is broken down into outcomes or performance criteria which describe what the learner needs to do to demonstrate competence in a particular area. Competence-based assessment became more widely used when NVQs were introduce in the 1980s. Learners were required to compile a portfolio of evidence against performance criteria, which was then assessed and verified within the organisation and externally.

Within competence-based assessment evidence of performance against criteria can come from a number of sources, all of which are valid methods of assessing competence.

Firstly, competence can be assessed through standard assignments or projects that are related to the subject area through the application of theory to practice. Students can also provide photographic evidence or video/audio recording to provide evidence to an assessor Other options include witness statements or observing a student in a work-based environment. To provide an example of this, some students will have part-time work that may provide evidence against competency in, for instance, customer service skills. A signed testimonial from a manager in the student's workplace can be used as evidence towards the assessment.

Activity

Consider the subject area that you teach. What types of assessment have you used recently?
Why did you choose that form of assessment?
Could you have done anything differently?
How did the assessment contribute to learner progress?

Principles of assessment

Although I do not intend to go into great depth on the principles of assessment, as there are many books out there that specialise in assessment that you could refer to (Gravells, 2009; Tummons, 2007), it is important to note that there are several principles that you need to be aware of when assessing your students.

Equity

As a practitioner and human being we can sometimes be subjective in our judgements and this can sometimes creep over into our assessment practices. However, as a professional we are duty bound to ensure that we are fair and equitable in our assessments and that all learners are treated equally when we make our judgments. Within your own organisation there will be guidelines on the assessment processes that you are required to conform to.

Validity

Validity is concerned with the extent to which the assessment matches or links to the requirements of the awarding body and the extent to which we are measuring what we say we are. A learner should not be penalised for spelling and grammar if the assessment was not designed to test that element of their knowledge.

Authenticity

Authenticity in assessment can have two distinct meanings. Firstly, is the assessment authentic, does it mirror the real world in which the student would be working? Secondly, is the work produced by the learner authentic? Is it their own? Have they copied it from a third party or source? Plagiarism has been and continues to be one of the most common problems with written work over the last 5–10 years. The rise of the internet and other associated e-technologies make it very difficult for us to determine whether a piece of work is authentic.

Sufficiency

We need to ensure that the assessments we produce provide sufficient coverage and depth of coverage to provide the evidence that our learners have achieved the set standard.

Reliability

Within assessments reliability is closely linked to accuracy and consistency. To ensure reliability we need to include moderation and cross-marking within our assessment processes to ensure that each assessor is working to the same standards.

Transparency

Do your learners know what they need to do to succeed? If you have a transparent system in place learners will understand what is required of them and the assessment will be closely linked to the outcomes of the course. This is particularly important when the assessments are summative assessments or the externally assessed assessments.

Assessment methods

When considering what types of assessment to use in our modules it is crucial to consider the most appropriate way of meeting the aims and learning outcomes of the course and the needs of our student body. We should also be cognisant of any additional support our learners may have. For example, should a student with severe dyslexia be required to provide written evidence if they can provide evidence orally or through a mini viva? The next section will briefly explore some of the options available to you when considering assessment.

Written assignments

These could be reports or essays designed to assess a learner's ability to grasp a particular concept. Both have advantages and disadavantages as methods. It could be argued that reports are more 'real-world' and use skills a learner will need as they move into their working lives, especially when it is a vocationally based curriculum. However, we need to ensure that we are clear in the purpose of a report when assessing a student. Conversely, essays can be used to assess a snapshot of learning and as a teacher it can provide an overview of a student's ability to identify key areas and points of a particular topic. The major disadvantage of essays in vocational education is the question of whether they are representative of what the learner will be doing when in employment.

Presentations

Presentations are invaluable to learners in that they provide them with some of the skills they will require in their working lives. They enable learners to gain confidence in their ability to speak publicly, and if presented jointly, will enable learners to develop group working and team-building skills.

Displays

Many vocational courses lend themselves to students creating a display or exhibition for peers or wider audiences. Displays can be as simple as poster presentations or as complex as fashion shows. Whatever level of complexity, this form of assessment can develop independent learning and thinking skills, alongside team-working and time management skills.

Exams

As a child raised on exams (both at Christmas and in the summer from the age of 11), I don't have any fears of being examined. However, I do question whether my ability to recite Ohms law or the periodic table has actually contributed to my career so far! In my opinion, and I respect that others may differ, an exam has no other purpose but to test memory and provide external bodies with statistics. That said, many courses do have externally set exams and as teachers we have a moral duty to ensure that our learners are prepared for this form of assessment and that they embrace them without fear.

Portfolios

These types of assessment allow a learner to show their development and progress over a period of time. Portfolios can be electronic as opposed to written, which may better suit our learners' learning styles. The main disadvantage is the perception that a portfolio can be a 'tick box' exercise.

Giving feedback

Effective student feedback is increasingly being recognised as a key influence on learning and student achievement.

Feedback is an essential part of assessment and is a two-way process that involves both the learner and the teacher. It is a form of communication that, if used effectively, can enhance and improve learning and help a learner's confidence through a process of scaffolding learning.

Good practice for giving feedback is that it should be positive, whether oral or written feedback. It should motivate learners, highlighting their areas of strength but at the same time providing some feed-forward for how they could improve and develop. I have always advocated a PIP approach – Positive, Improvement, Positive. Using this enables you as a teacher to create a feedback sandwich of positive encouragement filled with ideas and ways of improving. You should always use the learner's name too – this demonstrates that you value the effort they have put in. Comments which focus on how learners can improve encourage them to believe that they can improve. And surely this is the kind of classroom culture we should be trying to create: a culture of success in which every student can make achievements by building on their previous performance, rather than by being compared with others. We can promote such a culture by informing students about their strengths and weaknesses and by giving feedback about what their next steps should be. Suggestions for improvement should be focused on how students can close the gap between their current performance and the performance they are targeted to achieve, and be relevant to the lesson or unit and refer to the learning objectives.

An example of PIP feedback

This is a really interesting and well written piece of work Mary. You have captured all of the relevant details that the family would need to know before making a decision. I would suggest that you consider how you present this information, as at times it was quite confusing and as the reader there were areas that I wasn't sure of. Overall though this is a really positive start to the module and provides you with a strong basis for the rest of the year. Well done!

Probably the hardest decision to make about feedback is the amount to provide. A natural inclination is to want to 'fix' everything you see. That's the teacher's-eye view, where the target is perfect achievement of all learning goals. For real learning, what makes the difference is a usable amount of information that connects with something students already know and takes them from that point to the next level. Your feedback should give students a clear understanding of what to do next on a point or points that they can see they need to work on.

Feedback should also be timely – it needs to be provided whilst students are still mindful of the topic or assignment. My organisation has a three-week turnaround to provide feedback to students, and some would argue that this is still too long! As a general principle you should put yourselves in the learner's place. When would they most benefit from feedback? Certainly before they complete their next piece of assessed work, as good feedback will always include areas to improve upon.

Top tips for giving effective feedback

- Feedback should be clear and unambiguous.
- Feedback should be supportive and positive.
- Feedback should be provided in a timely fashion.
- Feedback should be developmental and include feed-forward.
- Feedback should scaffold learning.

Conclusion

In summary, this chapter has explored some of the principles and concepts of assessment. As teachers we will encounter different forms of assessment in our everyday life, some dictated by awarding bodies, but for much of what we do we have the ability to decide upon the most appropriate form of assessment for our learners. Having a repertoire of assessment methods allows us to make informed choices about formative and summative assessment formats and how we can address our students' needs whilst ensuring that what we do meets our own requirements for assessing progress. It is also important to note that giving feedback is an important part of the assessment process and one that should not be overlooked. Providing effective feedback requires time, but also careful thought and diplomacy. This chapter has considered some of the characteristics of good feedback and ways in which feedback can be constructed to motivate and encourage learners. The most important thing to remember is that feedback and assessment is a two-way dialogue and communication should be effective and timely.

References

Gravells, A. (2009) *Principles and Practice of Assessment in the Lifelong Learning Sector.* Exeter: Learning Matters.

Haywood, L.E. (2007) 'Curriculum, pedagogies and assessment in Scotland: the quest for social justice. "Ah kent yir faither"', *Assessment in Education: Principles, Policy and Practice*, Vol 14 (no 2), 251–268.

Tummons, J. (2007) *Assessing Learning in the Lifelong Learning Sector.* Exeter: Learning Matters.

Further reading

Scales, P. (2013) *Teaching in the Lifelong Learning Sector.* Maidenhead: Open University Press.

Technology-enhanced learning

Learning objectives

At the end of this chapter you will be able to:

- discuss some of the key debates around technology in the classroom;
- consider technology-enhanced learning (TEL) strategies;
- identify some of the resources available to you as a 14–19 teacher;
- discuss the advantages of technology within the classroom.

Introduction

Technology-enhanced learning (TEL) seeks to improve the student learning experience by:

- aiding student engagement, satisfaction and retention;

- helping to produce enterprising graduates with the skills required to compete in the global business environment;

- encouraging inspirational and innovative teaching;

- personalising learning that promotes reflection;

- delivering and supporting CPD and internationalisation.

The government's focus on TEL has greatly increased in recent years with a vision for the UK to become a world leader in education e-learning within the next ten years.

This chapter explores what we mean by technology-enhanced learning and how we as teachers can use technologies more effectively with our students. Traditionally, technology in the classroom has fallen into three key areas: e-learning, m-learning and blended learning, but as a resource technology can be much more than just a means to an end; the trick is to use it properly and effectively. We have all heard of, and probably suffered from, death by PowerPoint, and whilst there is a presumption that the introduction of technology into teaching and learning will always lead to improvement; there is no reason to believe this is necessarily the case. Using technology will not make a bad teacher good. An ineffective teacher with PowerPoint, assorted social media and online video clips will probably remain an ineffective teacher. The use of technology in education is about the effective use of tools to support and enhance. As a concept, technology for education can provide the teacher and the classroom with a wide array of tools, software, applications and processes that provide audio, images, animation, streaming video, satellite TV, CD-ROM, and computer-based learning, as well as local intranet/extranet and web-based resources. Technology-enhanced learning and e-learning can occur in or out of the classroom. It can be self-paced, asynchronous learning or may be instructor-led, synchronous learning. It is suited to distance learning and in conjunction with face-to-face teaching, which is termed 'blended learning'.

The following section will explore some of the definitions surrounding technology for learning.

E-learning

The Oxford English dictionary defines e-learning as 'Learning conducted via electronic media, typically on the Internet'. However the use of the letter 'e' in the term has led to e-learning being a confused concept. Kidd and Czerniawski (2010) suggest that the 'e' could have a wide range of meanings – enhanced learning, empowered learning, experiential learning and emergent learning to name but a few. As a strategy, e-learning processes can be described as synchronous (in real time), or asynchronous (out of real time).

Synchronous learning occurs in real time, with all participants interacting at the same time, while asynchronous learning is self-paced and allows participants to engage in the exchange of ideas or information without the dependency of other participants' involvement at the same time. As a concept, synchronous learning involves learners engaging with each other in online real time, for example face-to-face discussion through discussion boards, skype, virtual classrooms or chat rooms.

The concept of asynchronous learning is that learners do not all have to be online at the same time. It allows for learners to work at their own pace and could use technologies such as email, blogs, wikis, and discussion boards, as well as web-supported textbooks, hypertext documents, audio/video courses, and social networking.

The following list provides some examples of e-learning tools that can be used to support the traditional face-to-face activity, either synchronously or asynchronously:

- YouTube – YouTube is a video sharing website that can be used in the classroom to demonstrate a particular skill to students on any specific programme. It can also be used to set work for learners outside the classroom.
- Wiki – wikis can be used to encourage students to work collaboratively to build projects on a given topic.

- Blogs – blogs can be used to encourage learners to reflect and create e-portfolios and video diaries on their progress.

- Social media including Facebook and Twitter –very common social media where learners could set up study groups. However, you need to ensure that you as the teacher of the group takes responsibility for posts to ensure there is nothing that may cause offence or contravene any ethical or professional rules.

- Second Life – Second Life is a free 3D virtual world where users can socialise, connect and create using free voice- and text-chat. Simulations of work-related learning could be set up in Second Life as a learning tool for specific tasks.

Activity

Thinking about your teaching what resource/resources do you use that could be classed as e-learning technology or could be converted into e-learning technology?

M-learning

M-learning is perhaps a less well-known or -used term, but nevertheless one that exists within the range of learning technologies. M-learning can be defined as:

> *any sort of learning that happens when the learner is not at a fixed, pre-determined location.*
>
> *(Attewell and Savill-Smith, 2004: 2)*

The concept of M-learning is linked to the fact that the traditional classrooms in which we learn have changed and our students can now listen to lectures on mobile devices and research for projects whilst on the move. As a teacher this provides us with opportunities to utilise technology in different ways. For example, we can provide podcasts, use Facebook, Twitter or other social media to set tasks or send information. M-learning is asynchronous and is often used for distance-learning students, although it can be used to support the more traditional face-to face delivery methods.

MOOCS

MOOCS are massive online courses that are open to anyone. In addition to traditional technology-enhanced learning, such as pod-casts and filmed lectures, they offer interactive forums to provide real-time interaction between students and teachers. MOOCS are a relatively new concept, emerging as a popular method of learning in 2012. However, some critics believe they are now outdated – 'They came; they conquered very little; and now they face substantially diminished prospects.' (Zemsky, 2014: 57).

Blended learning

The definition of blended learning is a formal education programme in which a student learns, at least in part, through online learning, with some element of student control over time, place, path and/or pace; and in part in a supervised brick-and-mortar location away from home – the traditional classroom. The rise of virtual learning environments (VLEs) as a ubiquitous platform for hosting and delivering support materials means that for most students some minimal experience with blended learning is likely to already be the norm, at least in the context of UK education. Unfortunately, many teaching staff use the VLE as a repository for lecture notes and do not make full use of the learning opportunities it can provide. Four theories and models of blended learning exist in academic literature: flipped classroom, station rotation, flex model and lab rotation.

Flipped classroom

The term 'flipped' has become the pedagogical buzzword of the day – flipped learning, flipped classroom, flipped course currently seem to be the phrases mostly closely linked to technology-enhanced learning. The flipped classroom, or flipped learning, is a methodology, an approach to learning in which technology is employed to reverse the traditional role of classroom time. The fundamental foundation of the concept of flipped learning is active learning and the student-centred approach which emphasises 'learning by doing' (see Chapter 2).

If in the past classroom time has been spent lecturing to students, now, in a flipped model, this time is utilised to encourage individualised learning and provide one-on-one help to students, and to improve student–teacher interaction. The flipped classroom can have the benefit of being a more student-focused approach to teaching and learning. In terms of flexibility, students must be able to access equivalent content purely through online material – a challenge to institutions where the campus experience is a key part of the educational experience.

Station rotation model

'Station rotation' is an American term which, at its simplest, means that students rotate between different modes of learning. At least one of the modes should be online, but other activities can be group work, small projects or activities, tutoring or any other type of activity that is appropriate for the topic in question. This technique can be used as a whole-class activity or for smaller groupings within a larger group.

Lab rotation model

This is another American term, whereby students split their work between a normal classroom and a computer lab. It can be used effectively for project work where students go and research then come back to put their research into a format pre-determined by the teacher.

Flex model

The flex model is what is commonly described as online learning activity within the UK, where all learning is done online with tutor support through an online portal, skype or face-to-face.

Case study

The following is a case study of how technology-enhanced learning has increased student engagement within a well-known hotel management school. The author is a teacher at the school and is himself engaged in a Post Graduate Certificate in Education.

My institution and campus of work has implemented some significant changes in the past 12 months. Every student enrolled in the September 2014 semester onwards is to be given a tablet (iPad). In line with this decision, every facilitator, from the teaching faculty to the operation's staff that is involved in the practical side of teaching in our hospitality school, is also to be given an iPad. With the new tool in hand, the message from the management board is clear: facilitators should use this new tool to enhance the students' learning experience. In this regard, wouldn't students also expect lecturers to use the tablet and develop more interesting and interactive classes?

Additionally, the core structure of each teaching module has been altered. Originally each module was taught over 30 contact hours per semester. This was modified to 20 contact hours (in-class hours) and 10 non-contact hours (out-of-class hours). The term 'cloud hours' developed through discussions amongst the faculty when aiming to develop strategies of how to deliver the new course format. The term has now become part of our daily vocabulary. Throughout this study the expression 'cloud hours' will be used when referring to module hours that are used in the blended or flipped learning environment as opposed to the traditional class contact hours.

The table below shows the change taking one module as an example:

TABLE 5.1 Flipped approach example SEG

Structure before September 2014			Structure after September 2014		
In-class contact hours	Homework hours	Total hours	In-class contact hours	'Cloud hours'	Total hours
30	0 (at the discretion of the teacher, but not encouraged)	30	20	10 (encouraged as pre-work)	30

Having a touchscreen device for every student in school suggests a step in the right direction in increasing student engagement. The device helps students engage in their activities and

(continued)

(continued)

also promotes self-esteem, creates online learning communities and facilitates communication between the teachers and the students.

To look more closely at how mobile applications can be used to promote student engagement in cloud hours, it can be said that the greater involvement and effort of the student, as well as their comprehension of the module's language, suggests a positive influence on their engagement. The contribution by the academic institution and the social life outside of class hours will also impact the engagement outcomes in an encouraging manner. As for the lecturer, the comfort levels with the class delivery method as well as constant and prompt feedback are also regarded as influential on the engagement.

SHMS Leysin Campus is well positioned to encourage experiential learning. The students in the Hotel Management bachelor's programme have mandatory internships where every student gains industry experience. The same students also gain experience by living on campus, a former hotel. By exploiting these factors and allowing the students to incorporate them into their online learning experience the students are taking control of their learning outcomes and validating the experience. Some specific mobile applications such as 'HotelSims' (Hotelsims.com, 2015), or 'Leadership and Team Simulation: Everest' (Cb.hbsp.harvard.edu, 2015), strive to produce these exact effects. Encouraging students to engage in the cloud hours together over a specific topic where they have to make decisions based on their past and current experiences has a direct effect on the engagement in the module course. The students learn through their online communities and through their own resources. The simulators also offer constant and prompt feedback, not only from the facilitator but also from the mobile application that is directly linked to the students' involvement in the application.

In other words the more the student is working and using the simulators, the more feedback she or he will be receiving. The usage of mobile app simulators enriches the experience of the students, thus promoting more engagement. One of the other great benefits of mobile applications that can enhance student engagement concerns the communication aspect. Not only the communication between facilitator and student, but also the communication between the academic institution and the student, and the communication amongst students themselves.

This aspect enhances the campus social life, as well as the academic contribution to the students' life on campus. As previously mentioned, these are all characteristics contributing to the overall student engagement.

As for the academic contribution, moving away from emails and focusing on mobile applications that keep an up-to-date communication between the school and the students can also be seen as an advantage.

Most theories on student engagement appeared before the ideas of m-learning or e-learning, and this report suggests some ways in which we can bridge the gap between the two ages through mobile applications. The introduction of mobile application technology does not in itself recreate a new engagement, but rather applies engagement theories in a new way. Online learning communities (OLC) provide students with the possibilities of being involved in their own learning, promoting a deeper level of learning from their peers, notably from each other's successes and mistakes.

Online platforms encourage student self-centred learning, while the use of simulation applications foster experiential learning in a place where students can use their knowledge gained from experience and create new concepts. Research of self-centred learning from OLC could be developed further to investigate how students could create their own learning objectives and how they could evaluate themselves using mobile applications. Immediate or relatively prompt feedback from mobile applications keeps the engagement levels high. As suggested in different studies, this does imply a much higher engagement level and time availability from the facilitator. The question is how much are teachers willing to change their methods if this means more work and preparation?

Consider the following:

1   How could you incorporate cloud hours into your teaching?
2   How could you use specific technologies such as 'HotelSims' for your discipline area?

Is the use of technology appropriate for the 14–19 learner?

There is a perception within educational circles that everyone born from 1980 grew up immersed in computers and a wide range of IT technologies to such an extent that they became a generation different from their technologically impoverished forebears. Various terms were coined to describe these: Tapscott (1998) called them the Net Generation; Pelevin and Bromfield (2002) referred to them as Homo Zapiens. When I think back to my school days in the 1980s there was no internet and the new IT subjects that were starting to be introduced in schools were for the 'geeks' who understood binary and programming, not for the likes of me! I recall my first ever PC in 1993, an Amiga that had WordStar!

Prensky (2001) describes these people who were born into a technological age and learned to use all its devices regularly and naturally as 'digital natives', whereas I would be classed as a 'digital immigrant' who has tried, with varying degrees of success, to adapt to living in this new world. Crucially, many believe that 'digital immigrant' teachers are ill-equipped to meet the needs of their 'digitally native' students.

Prensky is of the opinion that, as learners, digital natives are likely to learn differently to previous generations and that we as teachers need to be aware of these differences when designing learning. Students today are growing up in a digital world, so educators need new approaches to make learning both real and relevant for today's students. He believes that:

- Digitally literate students specialise in content finding, analysis, and presentation via multiple media.

- Teachers specialise in guiding student learning, providing questions and context, designing instruction, and assessing quality.

- Administrators support, organise, and facilitate the process schoolwide.

- Technology becomes a tool that students use for learning essential skills and 'getting things done'.

The next section will consider some of the challenges that technology-enhanced learning and digital natives can create for the educator, and provide some ideas of how you can best use e-technology in your classroom.

Challenges and opportunities – making technology work for you

As teachers, the key to a good lesson is good planning. The internet can be an excellent resource for activities and lesson resources. Take a look at repositories that are set up for teachers. For example, the TES has an excellent repository with a wide range of activities, ideas and resources.

If your workplace uses interactive whiteboards (IWB) you will be able to create templates that allow you to display key learning points or objectives throughout the class. Most IWB software also has inbuilt functions and features that you can incorporate into your classroom. It is worth taking some time to familiarise yourself with IWBs as many teachers only use a fraction of their capability.

Most colleges and HEIs have adopted virtual learning environments within their organisations that both staff and students can use. In simple terms, a virtual learning environment (VLE) is a web-based platform for the digital aspects of courses of study. Common uses for VLEs include the ability to organise cohorts and groups; present resources, activities and interactions within a course structure; provide for the different stages of assessment; and most VLEs will link with the wider institution platforms for monitoring attendance, inputting results and reporting back to awarding bodies.

Activity

Consider your organisation. Does it host a VLE? How do you utilise its capability? Are there areas of the VLE that you could use better or start to use?!

Interactive voting systems as a tool

Interactive voting systems can be used in a variety of ways, from simple multiple-choice question-and- answer plenaries, to quizzes, game shows or whole-class revision of mock exam questions. They provide instant checks on student learning. At any stage of a lesson you can obtain instant feedback or change the focus of the lesson to review areas that the voting system highlights as troublesome.

Visualisers

Visualisers have been around for a long time, but they are getting cheaper and much more portable. They use a light and a digital camera and can be quickly linked to a digital projector. As well as showing objects they can be used to show work.

You can use the visualiser to show an example of a student's work to the whole class and carry out peer evaluation. A visualiser could also be used to enable students to produce their own animated short film.

PowerPoint

PowerPoint has become a very popular tool for the teacher, even though it was not originally designed for use in teaching. Excessive reliance on PowerPoint can stop teachers being teachers – becoming instead operators of technology and readers of slides.

The main criticism is that PowerPoint encourages, almost compels, teachers to adopt linear structures which, according to Kinchin, et al (2008: 333) '. . . have been related to passive, surface approaches to learning' rather than the development of higher level analysis and critical thinking.

The best use of PowerPoint is to provide a framework for the session. If there are things that you would regularly write on a whiteboard in more or less the same way, you could put them on to PowerPoint slide; the slides then become a backdrop to the session rather than the main focus of it. However, you need to ensure that you do not overuse this. Some teachers have a tendency to over-populate PowerPoint slides, so that rather than being a tool to enhance learning it becomes a script. The key to a good PowerPoint is to display key words and questions that enable you to discuss and expand on the topic.

PowerPoint can also be used successfully with an interactive whiteboard to add learners' points and convert them to text for additional notes.

Activity

Evaluate one of your own PowerPoint presentations or one of those developed by colleagues.

- How many slides are there? Do you need that many? (I would argue no more than 10–12 for an hour session.)
- Is it a 'framework' for the session or does it include most of the content? Can you discuss points or could a learner just read and gain as much not turning up?
- How busy are the slides? Is the font the right size? Do you need animations?
- Are the learners passive or does the presentation encourage discussion, enable questioning and assessment for learning opportunities?

Podcasting and vodcasting

If you are feeling creative, why not record some podcasts or vodcasts to help pupil understanding? You could even get the pupils to download podcasts or vodcasts to help them in the lesson. A simple podcast is a form of digital media that consists of a series of audio, video, or possibly radio and TV clips (licence permitting!).

Computers, tablets and mobile devices

Collaborative learning is a group-based learning approach in which learners are mutually engaged in a co-ordinated fashion to achieve a learning goal or complete a learning task. With recent developments in smartphone technology, the processing powers and storage capabilities of modern mobiles allow for advanced development and use of apps. Many app developers and education experts have been exploring smartphone and tablet apps as a medium for collaborative learning.

iPads as a teaching tool

In today's society most students have iPhones, iPads or one of the numerous android devices available on the market. There are so many educational apps for teachers released every month that even the most plugged-in educator would have a difficult time processing and utilising them all. Some of the most popular ones you may wish to explore are:

- 'ClassDojo' – a tool to help you manage the classroom, from managing behaviour to checking progress.
- Mind mapping apps such as 'Inkflow Visual' which provides a good platform for visual learning activities.
- Classroom voting apps that can be used for assessment activities, both formative and summative.
- Group work tasks can be managed with apps such as 'Trello' which enables students to work together on projects – perfect for events that you may wish to create for your learners.

Virtual classrooms

We have already discussed VLEs, which in turn can provide the opportunity to utilise a virtual classroom. A virtual classroom then allows learners to receive direct instruction from the teacher or trainer in an interactive environment. Learners can have direct and immediate access to their instructor for instant feedback and direction. The virtual classroom provides a structured schedule of classes, which can be helpful for students who may find the freedom of asynchronous learning to be overwhelming. In addition, the virtual classroom provides a social learning environment that replicates the traditional 'brick and mortar' classroom. Most virtual classroom applications provide a recording feature that allows instant playback for the learner, allowing them to progress at their own pace, catch up or simply review and revise.

Benefits of using technology in the classroom

When used effectively, technology can provide many advantages for the teacher and the learner. Using technology to provide real-world learning can give learners the opportunity to practise what they may not be able to in the classroom, or indeed provide apprentices with the opportunity to practise in cyberspace before working in the real world.

Modern educational technology can improve access to education and it can enable better integration for non-full-time students, particularly apprentices who are studying part time in a college environment. Learning material can be used for long-distance learning, or for students who are unable to attend any particular sessions. It therefore provides an opportunity for widening participation.

The use of educational apps generally has positive effect on learning. Pre- and post-use tests reveal that the use of apps on mobile devices can reduce the achievement gap between struggling and average students. Some educational apps improve group work by allowing students to receive feedback on answers and promoting collaboration in solving problems, which can then be linked to Personal Learning and Thinking skills (PLTS) and other skills that need to be incorporated into learning (see Chapter 6).

Disadvantages of technology

According to Bransford et al (1990: 115–141), 'technology does not guarantee effective learning', and inappropriate use of technology can even hinder it. With the internet and social media, using educational apps makes the students highly susceptible to distraction and sidetracking. Even though proper use has shown to increase student performances, being distracted would be detrimental. Another disadvantage is increased potential for cheating. Smartphones can be very easy to hide and use inconspicuously, especially if their use is normalised in the classroom. These disadvantages can be managed with strict rules and regulations on mobile phone use. We also need to be mindful of safeguarding around using internet and social media-based technologies.

Neil Postman endorsed the notion that technology impacts human cultures, including the culture of classrooms, and that this is a consideration even more important than considering the efficiency of a new technology as a tool for teaching. Regarding the computer's impact on education, Postman (1992) states:

> What we need to consider about the computer has nothing to do with its efficiency as a teaching tool. We need to know in what ways it is altering our conception of learning, and how in conjunction with television, it undermines the old idea of school.
>
> (Postman, 1992: 19)

Safeguarding the 14–19 learner

As technology develops, the internet and its range of services can be accessed through various devices including mobile phones, computers and game consoles. Although the internet has many positive uses, it provides the key method for the distribution of indecent images of children and young adults. We also need to be mindful about the potential for the grooming or radicalisation of young people, not to mention the potential for cyber bullying or trolling. Your organisation will have regulations in place around the use of technology for learning and will probably have some form of 'Acceptable ICT users policy'.

General good practice

It is often deemed inappropriate for teachers, tutors and trainers to communicate on a one to one basis with learners by:

- text message;
- email (other than the student's organisational email);
- instant messaging;
- or through social networking sites.

Should you be in a position where you need to do this it is advisable to include (where appropriate) a copy to a third party.

Text messages

Text messages are NOT the preferred method of communication between teaching staff and their learners. However where they are used, they should be group (bundled) messages, preferably from the organisation and should always be copied into the relevant safeguarding officer (for under 18s). In the event of an emergency, individual texts may be used but again should be copied into the safeguarding officer and/or parent.

Emails

Emails are a positive and simple method of communication between teachers and groups of learners and are easy to set up through VLEs. Group emails are preferred, and emails should never be sent to a learner's personal email account.

Social networking

Teachers should NOT have learners, especially those under the age of 18, as their 'friends' on social networking sites when the primary reason for the relationship is education and they have a position of trust in relation to that young person.

In summary

The presence and continuous growth of technology in every aspect of life in the 21st century has created a 'revolution' of the traditional teaching and learning experienced by past generations of students. As a tool, ICT enables a greater proportion of learners to access education, whereas traditionally they may have been in full-time work, or at the other end of the country. In addition using technology as part of your tool-kit can increase flexibility so that your student can access learning regardless of the time or their location. As a teacher it enables us to create interactive, stimulating materials when used correctly. However, as a note of caution, if used incorrectly it will hinder learning rather than enhancing it.

References

Attewell, J. & Savill-Smith, C. (2004) *Learning with Mobile Devices: Research and Development*. London: Learning and Skills Development Agency.

Bransford, J., Sherwood, R., Hasselbring, T., Kinzer, C. & Williams, S. (1990) 'Anchored instruction: why we need it and how technology can help'. In D. Nix & R. Spiro (eds) *Cognition, Education, and Multimedia: Exploring Ideas in High Technology*. Hillsdale, NJ: Lawrence Erlbaum.

Cb.hbsp.harvard.edu (2015) *Leadership and Team Simulation: Everest*. Available at: cb.hbsp.harvard.edu/cbmp/pages/demo/7000

Hotelsims.com (2015) *Hotel Simulations, Hotel Management Training and Certifications*. Available at: www.hotelsims.com

Kidd, W. & Czerniawski, G. (2010) *Successful Teaching 14–19: Theory, Practice and Reflection*. London: Sage.

Kinchin, G, Hay, D. B., Harvey, E. & Wells, I M. (2007) 'Quantitative and qualitative measures of student learning', *Higher Education*, 56 (2), 221–239.

Pelevin, V. & Bromfield, A. (2002) *Homo Zapiens*. New York: Viking.

Postman, N. (1992) *Technopoly: The Surrender of Culture to Technology*. New York: Vintage Books.

Prensky, M. (2001). *Digital Natives, Digital Immigrants*, MCB University Press, Vol 9(5).

Tapscott, D. (1998) *Growing Up Digital: The Rise of the Net Generation*. New York: McGraw-Hill.

Zemsky, P. (2014). 'With a MOOC MOOC here and a MOOC MOOC there, here a MOOC, there a MOOC, everywhere a MOOC MOOC'. *Journal of General Education*, Vol 63(4).

Further Reading

www.newteachers.tes.co.uk/content/make-most-ict-your-classroom (accessed 8 September 2015).

Making 14–19 work

Functional skills and PLTS

Learning objectives

After studying this chapter you will be able to:

- define functional skills;
- explain the historical context of functional skills;
- identify activities that you could use to embed functional skills in the 14–19 curriculum;
- define Personal Learning and Thinking Skills (PLTS) within 14–19 education;
- describe some of the activities that can be used to demonstrate PLTS skills in the classroom.

Introduction

This chapter will explore some of the skills that are crucial within 14–19 education, namely functional skills and Personal Learning and Thinking skills (PLTS). It will provide an overview of the skills and how you as a 14–19 teacher can embed them within your classroom.

Functional skills

Functional skills are practical skills in English, mathematics and ICT that enable learners to deal with practical problems and challenges. They are defined as the skills that 'enable everyone to work confidently, effectively and independently in life and at work' (www.aqa.org, accessed 26 September 2015).

They were piloted in the UK in 2007 as part of the development of the Diploma qualification which was introduced in 2008. Functional skills are an essential part of the secondary curriculum and are embedded in the revised Programmes of Study for English, mathematics and ICT at Key Stage 3 and Key Stage 4, and in the revised GCSE subject criteria for these subjects. They are also available as stand-alone qualifications for young people and adults.

Functional skills are available at entry levels 1–3, levels 1 and 2.

A brief history of functional skills

Functional skills were developed following the publication of the 14–19 Education and Skills White Paper (February 2005) and the Skills White Paper (March 2005), in response to employment needs and employer requests to provide a workforce that is competent and able to compete in an ever increasing competitive environment. They were piloted in 2007, and following a three year pilot the first full teaching of them commenced in 2010. During their pilot and development the then Labour government plans were that all young people would need to achieve functional skills at level 2 in order to be awarded a GCSE at grade C or above in the subject.

Rationale for functional skills

The Government suggests that functional skills are a key to success. They open doors to learning, to life and to work. Functional skills are valued by employers and further education and are a platform on which to build other employability skills. Better functional skills can mean a better future – as learners or as employees.

For example, they help us recognise good-value deals when making purchases, write an effective application letter, or use the internet.

In essence, functional skills are practical skills for every day work in English, mathematics and ICT, and the underlying philosophy of functional skills is that with them a learner will have the ability to select the right English, maths or ICT skills to solve different problems. An example of being functional in maths would be the ability to understand a wage slip and being able to plan a journey using public transport.

The term 'functional skills' relates to England only. Elsewhere in the UK the equivalents are: Essential Skills Wales, Core Skills in Scotland and Essential Skills in Northern Ireland.

So how are functional skills different to key skills, basic skills, skills for life and core skills, which are other skill bases you may come across within the English system?

To answer that question we will first have to look at these other skills.

Key skills

Key skills are defined as, 'essential, generic skills which are the basis of all successful lifelong learning and development' Scales (2008: 253). They were originally introduced following the Dearing review of post-16 education in 1996. They consist of six key skills, with each of the skills being available at levels 1–4. To be successful the learner must produce a portfolio and pass an external test. The key skills currently in existence are:

- Communication
- Application of number
- Information technology
- Improving own learning and performance
- Working with others
- Problem solving

Basic skills

Basic skills were derived from the government report *A Fresh Start* (Moser, 1999), more commonly known as the Moser report. This report suggested that at least 7 million adults had literacy and numeracy levels at or below those expected of 11-year olds. Following this report the government launched the Skills for Life strategy which included standards for literacy and numeracy programmes, with five levels being available, entry levels 1–3, level 1 (foundation) and level 2 (intermediate).

Basic skills were defined by the Basic Skills Agency as, 'the ability to read, write and speak in English/Welsh and to use mathematics at a level necessary to progress at work and in society in general'.

Skills for life

The term 'skills for life' tends to be used synonymously with basic skills, and are the skills referred to by the skills strategy as being those required to up-skill our workforce. Skills for life tend to be aimed at the adult learner whereas the key skills framework tends to be aimed at the 14–19-year-old market.

Core skills

Core skills mean different things to different professions. In England the common core skills are English, number, digital and employability skills (including teamwork, and problem-solving skills), commonly listed as; Working with Others, Communication, Numeracy, Problem Solving and Information Technology. These are covered from Access 3 to Higher level and are usually embedded within qualifications.

Teaching functional skills

As a teacher you need to be aware that functional skills are not separate curriculum subjects but an important element of the teaching and learning of all subjects. In developing functional skills, learners can adapt and apply what they have learned to suit different situations that face them. Teaching and learning of functional skills can be through a range of models, from discrete lessons to fully embedding teaching and learning. However, it is expected that in the long term, functional skills will remain the responsibility of core subject teachers, but will be reinforced throughout the rest of the curriculum in every lesson.

To teach functional skills effectively you need to develop the applied skills in your learners. For some of you, this is simply formalising your existing teaching approach. Functional English, mathematics and ICT help learners reinforce skills in communication, problem solving, listening, time management and team-working – a solid foundation for further learning and employment, and as the qualifications are designed to help learners become more confident there is an entitlement to study functional stills to age 19.

Functional skills teaching should build on existing good practice that has been developed from key and adult basic skills teaching. All models of delivery have merit. However, reinforcement across the curriculum is the desired goal, with specialist input where required. Helping learners to become more functional has significant implications for learning and teaching and will require the teacher to develop and build upon their existing practices for example:

- Applied learning
- Problem-centred learning
- Assessment for learning

Within any organisation there will be two broad groups of staff involved in functional skills delivery:

- The English, mathematics, and ICT specialists, who have direct responsibility for assessment, planning programmes and teaching functional skills, and the specialist teachers of vocational subjects, who have responsibility for teaching English, mathematics and ICT alongside their specialist subject. Note though that ICT teachers do not require a subject-specific teaching qualification.
- All other staff who have a responsibility for generally supporting the development of English, mathematics and ICT skills and provide opportunities to practise them in their own area of learning or vocational area.

At the time of writing there are no specific requirements for teaching functional skills. The current requirements for teaching in the FE and skills sector apply – i.e. Diploma in Education and Training (DET) or a Postgraduate Certificate in Education (PGCE) in relevant subject areas. It is for provider organisations to assure themselves that teachers have appropriate levels of subject competence. Skills for Life teaching qualifications in literacy, ESOL or numeracy indicate that the teacher has the right skills and teaching expertise to teach functional skills in English or mathematics.

Other people supporting learners on functional skills programmes, for example, assessors and learning support practitioners would benefit from additional training to support learners on functional skills programmes.

A suite of functional skills CPD programmes, developed and piloted in 2012, can be found on the Excellence Gateway: www.toolkits.excellencegateway.org. uk/functional-skills-starter-kit/section-3-developing-effective-practice/teaching-approaches-and-models-delivery#sthash.a1Sq2RYn.dpuf

Teaching and learning in functional skills

As previously discussed, functional skills should enable learners to solve problems in any given situation, and therefore as a teacher we need to be mindful that any activities we provide in the classroom allows freedom of choice for the learner.

The following section, whilst not exhaustive, provides some ideas for using functional skills within a classroom environment.

Functional English skills

Arguably English is one of the easiest skills to embed in teaching as we use English as a form of communication on a daily basis, whether written, verbal or reading.

Depending upon the subject you are teaching there are many options for English – role play, designing and producing posters, interviewing fellow students and staff about a particular topic, or reading and summarising a piece of text. All of these could be rolled up into one activity. For example, teaching travel and tourism, a role play of the booking of a holiday could include a conversation with a customer to identify their requirements, reading brochures and summarising information back to the customer then providing a leaflet on possible choices. There are also opportunities for role play activities using the telephone as an assessment tool for communication.

Activity

Consider your subject area, how could you embed English as a functional skill into your classes?

Maths

Maths again is a relatively easy skill to include in your classroom. It occurs in so many different parts of our daily lives that you can embed it into your teaching without anyone actually realising they are doing maths. The trick is to avoid using the word maths! Again, using travel and tourism as subject area, there are many different activities that you can do in the classroom, or indeed the learner can undertake in work-placement or work-simulation. Building upon the communication of providing a family with holiday options you could now build into your class the next layer of information the family may require. You can get students to cost the holiday from the brochure manually. They can then create a graph of resort temperature and hours of sunshine, working out average temperatures for any given month. There are also options to include working out flight times and converting currency from British pounds into the currency of the destination. All of which can be embedded as a fun activity.

Activity

Consider your subject area, what activities can you embed that provide opportunities for functional maths?

ICT

Technology is the fastest growing skill of all, and quite probably the one that your learners are more skilled at than you are! Traditionally, ICT skills have been based around students developing spreadsheets, or other types of data. However, with the rise of social media, iPhones and messenger, plus the many other apps that will have been developed since this was written, there are many more opportunities to embed ICT in your subject. Learners like the opportunity to be able to use new technology so to embed ICT skills I would suggest that you explore some of the new concepts available to you. Facebook and Twitter are two social media apps that you can use to engage your learners whilst also advocating safety and security.

Activity

Twitter as a social media application is very popular in today's society. Is this a function that you could use in your subject area? How effective would any learning be from using Twitter? Are there any other social media applications that you could use?

Functional skills standards

Standards for functional skills were first introduced in 2007 as draft standards to accompany the pilot. The standards simply set out the skill required and the types of activities that may provide evidence of proficiency against the skill. The level of proficiency is determined by the learner's ability to apply the skill to everyday situations. The current standards can be found on the government web pages (www.gov.uk).

Other methods of functional skill delivery

Whilst the previous section dealt with the embedding of functional skills into the curriculum, which is usually taught by the subject teacher, not all functional skills are embedded. The argument for this is that learners should be able to apply their learning to everyday life and other areas, and therefore some organisations use other methods to teach functional skills.

Discrete

In this approach the functional skills are delivered entirely by specialists and delivered separately from the main qualification. Whilst this has advantages in that it enables a specialist to teach skills that in theory can be applied to any situation, it also has major disadvantages in that your learners may see it as 'extra maths' or 'extra English'. In my experience this approach does demotivate and deter learners who have chosen to study engineering, hospitality or any other subject area and find themselves in 'maths lessons'!

Partly embedded

Here the functional skills are still taught by specialists but are applied across a range of subjects. This could involve the specialist working with a range of different disciplines and teaching the skill discretely from the subject but then liaising with the subject tutors to ensure that they apply the process to the subject. For example, the functional skills specialist may teach percentages and this is then used in the vocational area as a topic in any given session.

Mostly embedded

Here the skills are taught by specialists but are reinforced and applied in context across the subject areas. The specialist in effect teaches within the subject area and uses the subject area as a basis for examples and practical application.

Fully embedded

Fully embedded functional skills are taught by teachers within the subject area through naturally occurring opportunities within the context of the principal learning (as discussed in a previous section).

Case study: discrete delivery

College X delivers functional skills to its learners on a discrete basis. Each learner has two hours taught classes for each functional skill per week. In the classes the learners are given a problem to solve. Each learner must then produce a plan of how they intend to solve the problem, complete the plan, check the findings and produce a report on the findings together with an evaluation of the process. The college believes that delivery in this way enables the learners to master the skills and transfer the mastery to any context.

What are the advantages and disadvantages of this method for your organisation?

How do you think the learners will react to two hours of 'maths, english, ICT'?

To help you further with ideas visit the following:

www.tes.co.uk/teaching-resource/functional-skills-resources

Assessment of functional skills

Functional skills are assessed externally by the awarding body in question. Each awarding body will offer their own assessments for each of the functional skills on offer and as a teacher you are able to access any of the websites to look at sample papers. This website provides examples of English assessments at various levels: www.nocn.org.uk/functional_skills_sample_assessments_english/fs_sa_-_en_-_re (accessed 21 November, 2015).

At the time of writing one of the awarding bodies had developed an on-screen assessment for their ICT functional skills, which I am sure will be replicated as technology continues to develop. The awarding body in question uses an on-screen testing system that allows learners to engage with the process online, complete tasks and upload their responses and completed documents. Benefits of the system are billed as:

- an on-screen, self-contained test with no need to retrieve or prepare data files in advance, print or retain learner evidence, or manage local email accounts;

- the use of familiar MS Office applications (for example, Word and Excel) to complete key tasks;

- on-screen assessments that can be scheduled on demand and booked up to 30 minutes prior to the assessment;

- assessments that can be downloaded to a laptop in advance and taken with or without a live internet connection.

Documentation from the government states that the assessment for functional skills must be consistent with the levels set out in the skills standards and with the associated coverage and range specified within the functional skills subject criteria. In addition, it must:

- provide realistic contexts, scenarios and problems;
- specify tasks that are relevant to the context;
- require application of knowledge, skills and understanding for a purpose;
- require problem solving.

(Criteria for Functional Skills Qualifications, Ofqual 2012)

The level of difficulty for functional skills assessment must be determined by the following interacting factors:

- the complexity of tasks/problems and the contexts within which they are embedded;
- the technical demand of the content that might be applied in these contexts;
- a learner's level of familiarity with the type of task/problem and context;
- the level of independence required of the learner.

Core skills Scotland

The equivalent of functional skills in Scotland are core skills. The core skills are a group of five skills that have been identified by employers as most likely to be needed in a work environment and are key to learning and working in today's world. They are: Communication, Numeracy, Information and Communication Technology, Problem Solving and Working with Others. Each core skill is available at levels 2–6 of the Scottish Credit and Qualifications Framework (SCQF).

Essential skills Wales (ESW)

The essential skills Wales are very similar to the English functional skills, being English, mathematics and ICT, available from level 1 to level 4. ESW has been in place in the Welsh system since 2010, when they superseded key skills.

ESW content, structure and assessment was reviewed through comprehensive stakeholder engagement in 2013 – with new qualifications trialled in 2014. ICT was replaced by a new Digital Literacy qualification.

Essential skills Northern Ireland

The Department for Employment and Learning (DEL) launched the Essential Skills for Living Strategy and action plan in April 2002. The Essential Skills for

Living Strategy aims to improve adult literacy and numeracy (and now ICT) in Northern Ireland. The Essential Skills qualifications are intended for anyone over the age of 16 in Northern Ireland who wants to improve their literacy, numeracy or ICT skills to help get a job or get on in life.

They are taken in almost all forms of post-16 learning, including Apprenticeships and Training for Success, where learners have not already achieved GCSEs in English, mathematics or ICT at grades A*–C.

Personal thinking and learning skills (PLTS)

The aims of the PLTS curriculum is that young people should become successful learners, confident individuals and responsible citizens. The development of PLTS is an essential part of meeting these aims. PLTS have considerable impact on young people's ability to enter work and adult life as confident and capable individuals who can make a positive contribution to society.

Careful planning is necessary to ensure that PLTS are successfully integrated. Across the 14–19 sector, whether that be school, college or a learner on an apprenticeship, all learners should have the opportunity to plan and complete tasks in real settings or simulated work-based environments,

The six areas of PLTS are:

- Independent enquirers
- Creative thinkers
- Reflective learners
- Team workers
- Self-managers
- Effective participators

For each group of skills, a focus statement sums up the range of skills. This is accompanied by a set of outcome statements that are indicative of the skills, behaviours and personal qualities associated with each group. Each group is distinctive and coherent. The groups are also interconnected. Learners are likely to encounter skills from several groups in any one learning experience. For example, independent enquirers set goals for their research with clear success criteria (reflective learners) and organise and manage their time and resources effectively to achieve these goals (self-manager). In order to acquire and develop fundamental concepts such as organising oneself, managing change, taking responsibility and perseverance, learners will need to apply skills from all six groups in a wide range of occupational and learning contexts.

1 Independent enquirers

Focus:

Individuals process and evaluate information in their investigations, planning what to do and how to go about it. They take informed and well-reasoned decisions, recognising that others have different beliefs and attitudes.

Individuals:

- identify questions to answer and problems to resolve
- plan and carry out research, appreciating the consequences of decisions
- explore issues, events or problems from different perspectives
- analyse and evaluate information, judging its relevance and value
- Consider the influence of circumstances, beliefs and feelings on decisions and events
- support conclusions, using reasoned arguments and evidence.

2 Creative thinkers

Focus:

Individuals think creatively by generating and exploring ideas, making original connections. They try different ways to tackle a problem, working with others to find imaginative solutions and outcomes that are of value.

Individuals:

- generate ideas, explore possibilities and ask questions to extend their thinking
- connect their own and others' ideas and experiences in inventive ways
- question their own and others' assumptions
- try out alternatives or new solutions and follow ideas through
- adapt ideas as circumstances change.

3 Reflective learners

Focus:

Individuals evaluate their strengths and limitations, setting themselves realistic goals with criteria for success. They monitor their own performance and progress, inviting feedback from others and making changes to further their learning.

Individuals:

- assess themselves and others, identifying opportunities and achievements
- set goals with success criteria for their development and work
- review progress, acting on the outcomes
- invite feedback and deal positively with praise, setbacks and criticism
- evaluate experiences and learning to inform future progress
- communicate their learning in relevant ways for different audiences.

4 Team work

Focus:

Individuals work confidently with others, adapting to different contexts and taking responsibility for their own part. They form collaborative relationships, resolving issues to reach agreed outcomes.

Individuals:

- collaborate with others to work towards common goals
- reach agreements, managing discussions to achieve results
- adapt behaviour to suit different roles and situations, including leadership roles
- show fairness and consideration to others
- take responsibility, showing confidence in themselves and their contribution
- provide constructive support and feedback to others.

5 Self-managers

Focus:

Individuals organise themselves, showing personal responsibility, initiative, creativity and enterprise with a commitment to learn and self-improvement. They actively embrace change, responding positively to new priorities, coping with challenges and looking for opportunities.

Individuals:

- seek out challenges or new responsibilities and show flexibility when priorities change
- work towards goals, showing initiative, commitment and perseverance
- organise time and resources, including personal and work-related demands
- respond positively to change, seeking advice and support when needed
- manage their emotions, build and maintain relationships.

6 Effective participators

Focus:

Individuals actively engage with issues that affect them and those around them. They play a full part in the life of their school, college, workplace or wider community by taking responsible action to bring improvements for others as well as themselves.

Individuals:

- discuss issues of concern, seeking resolution where needed
- present a persuasive case for action
- propose practical ways forward, breaking these down into manageable steps
- identify improvements that would benefit others as well as themselves
- try to influence others, negotiating and balancing diverse views to reach workable solutions
- act as an advocate for views and beliefs that may differ from their own.

FIGURE 6.1 Personal learning and thinking skills

Assessing for PLTS

The following section provides some examples of how you might assess PLTS.

Case study

Trevor works at a local training provider assessing apprenticeships within the engineering framework. Units within the apprenticeship framework should include clear and appropriate integrated opportunities for developing and applying PLTS within the assessment criteria and PLTS should be integrated within the assessment criteria to explicitly recognise the application of these skills in sector-related contexts.

While PLTS will have to be formally assessed in an apprenticeship, they do not have to be accredited. PLTS should be recorded as part of the apprentice's portfolio and cross references should be made to any supporting evidence to demonstrate the effective application of the referenced elements of the skill.

Trevor provides a guide for his students and their employers to explain what PLTS are and to give them examples of how they can provide evidence against the six PLTS skills. The following is an extract from his guide.

Introduction for the apprentice

Personal, Learning and Thinking Skills (PLTS) describe the qualities and skills required for success in learning and life and are comprised of six groups of skills which, within an apprenticeship framework, must be assessed. Learners will have opportunities to develop, apply and assess all the personal, learning and thinking skills within their chosen intermediate apprenticeship/advanced apprenticeship framework. The six PLTS are:

- Independent enquirers
- Creative thinkers
- Reflective learners
- Team workers
- Self-managers
- Effective participators

Here are some examples of how you can provide evidence within your portfolio against these skills.

Independent enquirers

Provide an example of a time you read a book or researched the internet for information to help you make a decision.

a   What did you research?
b   How did you use the information to make a decision?
c   What were the consequences of your decision?

For example:

> *At work I had to research manual handling as I had to lift a lot of heavy objects. I learnt that if you don't bend your knees then you could seriously damage your back. I now always bend my knees when I lift heavy objects as I am aware of the consequences of not lifting properly.*

<u>Self-managers</u>

Provide an example of when you have had to work to a goal, showing commitment, perseverance and initiative.

a   Think of goal or challenge. Have you ever worked on it yourself (i.e researched it at home without it being part of your assessment)?
     How did you demonstrate initiative?

For example:

> *I was set a task at work that had to be completed in five days. I worked out a project plan the night before so that I could make sure I had enough time for all of the tasks I needed to do complete on time.*

Provide an example of how you have planned for and managed risks.

a   Think of a risk at work that you know you have to take.
b   Write down what the risk is, why you have to take it and how you manage the risk (don't forget PPE!).

For Example:

> *I was asked to wire brush and grind down an engine bay. I anticipated that there would be a lot of debris so I tried to minimise this by hoovering first and making sure I wore protective eye goggles.*

Think about your subject area and develop a guide for students to assess their PLTS within the working context.

Conclusions

In summary, all 14–19 learning will include the addition of several skills sets designed to provide the learner with the skills they need to be effective in the workplace and in wider society. Functional skills are essential skills and key to providing employability skills to our learners. They are available at a range of levels, and as teachers we should consider how we can best support them in our classroom, whether that is through discrete delivery or through embedded delivery

within our own subject area. Personal learning and thinking skills are also important for our learners, and again as teachers we have the opportunity to embed them
into our teaching, or the workplace, as with the apprenticeship frameworks.

References

Moser, C. (1999) *A Fresh Start*. London: DfEE.
Scales, D. (2008). *Teaching in the Lifelong Learning Sector*. London: Open University
    Press.
Ofqual (2012) *Criteria for Functional Skills Qualifications*. Richmond, Surrey: Ofqual.

Further reading

www.dfes.gov.uk/keyskills
www.dfes.gov.uk/readwriteplus
www.qca.org.uk/functionalskills
www.totallyskilled.co.uk

Coaching and mentoring in the 14–19 sector

Introduction

Coaching and mentoring are development techniques based on the use of one-to-one discussions to enhance an individual's skills, knowledge or work performance. This chapter will explore some of the definitions of coaching and mentoring and consider how they could be used to best effect with the 14–19 learner.

What is mentoring?

Mentoring involves the use of the same models and skills of questioning, listening, clarifying and reframing associated with coaching. Traditionally, however, mentoring has tended to describe a relationship in which a more experienced colleague uses his or her greater knowledge and understanding of the work or workplace to support the development of a more junior or inexperienced member of staff.

One key distinction is that mentoring relationships tend to be longer term than coaching arrangements. In simple terms, mentoring is a process that creates relationships between experienced and less experienced people with a view to helping the less experienced person to develop. Other published definitions follow similar themes to this, with Pollard defining mentoring as:

The provision of support for the learning of one person through the guidance of another person, who is more skilled, knowledgeable and experienced in relation to the context of the learning taking place.

(Pollard et al, 1997: 19)

In summary, a mentor is someone available to learn from.

Mentoring is a valuable strategy that teachers can use to provide students with the emotional, pastoral and academic support that they need to achieve their goal, whether that be the completion of a particular task or assignment, completion of the programme or transition into the workplace. Through the provision of information, guidance, and encouragement, mentors can play an important role in nurturing students' aspirations.

Mentoring can serve many different purposes, quite often linked to the individual's personal characteristics, attributes, age and needs. Within 14–19 education it could be argued that the mentoring role should focus on developing the knowledge, competencies, and confidence students need to successfully undertake their responsibilities and prepare them for work. In addition, mentors can also help students with their external environment, family, home situation, or just being a teenager. However, as a note of caution teachers should not assume sole responsibility for their learner, but instead should know where to signpost them to if specialist help is required.

Informal mentoring for the 14–19 learner

Within informal mentoring, relationships are formed with older and more experienced individuals such as parents, extended family members, neighbours, teachers, ministers and others with whom students have regular contact.

Informal mentoring involves the provision of general guidance and support and, in some instances, helping a student learn something new. It also promotes students' sense of well-being by challenging the negative opinions they may have of themselves and demonstrating that they can have positive relationships with adults (Rhodes, Grossman and Resch, 2000).

An informal relationship may be short or longterm, but in both instances can have a lasting positive impact on the student. Informal mentoring relationships are far more common than formal ones.

Formal mentoring

Formal mentoring involves a structured and intentional approach to offering students those experiences and benefits similar to the ones provided by informal mentors. Such initiatives are often facilitated by course managers as part of student support systems and encompass both one-on-one relationships between an adult and the student, or an older, more experienced peer and a younger peer, as well as small groups of students working with an adult or older peer on a particular goal. In all instances, mentoring activities take place at regularly scheduled times over an extended period, and are most often only one component of a comprehensive program. For the 14–19 sector formal mentoring can have positive outcomes for some of the less appropriate behaviours that can occur in this age group. For example, poor attendance, poor performance or external issues such as drug use, bullying, sexual exploitation or radicalisation. Formal mentoring systems can be school- or college-based, community-based, and occasionally workplace-based.

Activity

Think about your organisation. What formal mentoring schemes are in place for your students to access? Are there opportunities to expand these and create peer mentoring networks?

Mentoring skills

As a mentor there are many different ways in which you could support your learners. Clutterbuck, (1985) identified a four-dimensional grid, or positioning map, reproduced below, to identify four key areas of support that you could engage with. Mentors can position themselves in one of four quadrants, between directive and non-directive, challenging and supportive. The mentor's position may change from student to student, depending upon their own personal needs. For example, you may have a student who has very little self-confidence in their own ability who needs structured support. For this student you as a mentor

FIGURE 7.1 Four dimensions of mentoring

Adapted from Clutterbuck, 1985

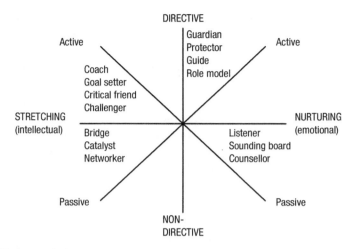

FIGURE 7.2 Skills for mentoring

Adapted from Klasen and Clutterbuck, 2002

would fall in the supportive, directive quadrant. In contrast you may find your-self working with a student who is very able but lazy and not very receptive to authoritarian approaches. This student may be more challenging to work with but I would suggest that you would be in the challenging, non-directive quadrant and facilitate learning.

Activity

Consider your cohort of learners. Can you identify the type of mentor you need to be with them? Are there some students who fall into more than one category?

This basic tool has been extended further to provide examples of the skills that each quadrant requires for the mentor to be effective. In addition, the quadrants have been changed slightly to read, stretch and nurture rather than challenge and support.

Mentoring styles

Within the Klasen and Clutterbuck model there are different approaches that you can consider for each of the quadrants. The first of these is to adopt a telling style. Telling falls within the directive section of the model, and whilst sometimes nec-essary isn't always appropriate for a mentoring approach as it moves the learning from an active student-centered approach to a passive approach.

The second style is that of advisor, and whilst this is still a directive approach it allows the learner to be involved in the learning through making decisions and taking action based upon advice received. This approach can be tempered to be less directive as learners gain more confidence in their abilities.

The third style is the developmental style. Developmental mentoring is non-directive and its primary function is to support self-directed learning and encourage the learner to explore options and develop their own resources and solutions.

There are four key elements for a non-directive style:

- asking questions rather than telling;

- encouraging the learner to talk;

- empowering the learner to think things through themselves;

- letting the learner find their own solution.

Whilst most people have a style of helping they are more comfortable with, it is also important that the style of helping is appropriate both for the situation and the needs of the learner. It is therefore useful to demonstrate flexibility in the style of help offered and to develop skills in order to advise and to use the non-directive developmental helping styles. Try to develop an awareness of your own preferred helping styles and be mindful of whether these preferred styles are the most appropriate to the situation.

Mentoring relationships

The most successful mentor relationships are relationships which are two-way, both mentor and mentee preparing for and committing to the process.

In addition, the mentor and mentee need to be appropriately matched, without any interpersonal issues. This may be a challenge with some of your learners who find it difficult relating to an adult mentor.

There are two broad types of mentoring relationships, as previously discussed: formal and informal. In addition to these broad types, there are also peer, situational and supervisory mentoring relationships.

Characteristics of a mentor

An effective mentor will help their mentee recognise their own abilities and limitations, whilst at the same time challenging and encouraging them in their studies. Research published in 2004 identified several different characteristics of a mentor. These characteristics are divided into eight distinct areas and are reproduced here in full, together with a description of what it means in practice for you as the mentor and for the person you are mentoring.

TABLE 7.1 Mentoring characteristics

Defining characteristic	
Authentic	Genuine, fair, honest, supportive, understanding, loyal, helpful, principled, thoughtful, respectful and empowering of others.
Nurturing	Kind, sensitive, compassionate, easy-going, spiritual, patient, generous and empathetic to others.
Approachable	Humorous, friendly, encouraging, communicative, positive, open, caring, co-operative and considerate of others.
Competent	Knowledgeable, bright, interested, intelligent, enthusiastic, professional, confident, experienced, insightful and informative to others.
Conscientious	Efficient, organised, disciplined, consistent, strict, and available to others.
Hard-working	Dedicated, motivated, committed, ambitious, energetic, driven, and workaholics who tend to be demanding of self and others.
Inspirational	Risk-taking, visioning, inspiring, creative, curious, dynamic, strong, passionate, direct, brilliant, challenging and assertive.
Volatile	Neurotic, overbearing, egocentric, outrageous, vindictive, contradictory, self-centred, wild, eccentric, opinionated, stressed, cunning, hard and picky.

Darwin, 2004

Activity

Consider Darwin's list of attributes and characteristics. How does this list compare to your own skills? What professional development needs do you have in order to be an effective mentor?

Options for mentoring the 14–19 learner

One-on-one mentoring

The one-on-one model of mentoring is individualised and personal. This model is excellent for developing a good relationship. However, the model offers only one point of view and may not meet the mentee's needs if the mentor is not well versed in all of the mentee's areas of interest or there are other conflicts such as personal conflicts. I am sure we have all heard our students say things such as 'I find him/her difficult to talk to'.

Team mentoring

The collaborative nature of team mentoring removes some of the potential conflicts of interests found with the one-to-one model. The mentee has access to different points of view and to discussions amongst course team members. This model may be appropriate if the learner finds advice conflicting as it allows them to sit down and discuss things with more than one tutor.

Multiple mentors

In this model, the mentee has more than one mentor, and the mentors all meet individually with the mentee rather than jointly (as is the case with team mentoring). In this model a learner could have mentors from across discipline areas and settings. For example, they may have a work-based mentor, a college-based mentor within the subject area and a different mentor supporting them on a pastoral basis. Having ready access to multiple mentors from different disciplines can be an ideal source of advice and guidance for a learner.

Distance mentoring

Mentoring via e–mail, supplemented by telephone calls and occasional visits, can be highly effective for mentees with mentors at different institutions, especially if learners are on day release from an apprenticeship or similar. Distance mentoring can be a convenient way to work with a mentor or mentee, but you have to trust that messages are received and acted upon. If the message is not carefully communicated, recipients can misunderstand the message or its tone and react in a way that is not expected by the writer. If a relationship has already been established between mentor and mentee, this method of mentoring may be more effective.

Peer mentoring

As a process, peer mentoring is a scheme that allows learners to help each other with their problems, either work-related or within the school or college itself. Schools and colleges that have peer mentoring schemes in place use them as a means of improving behaviour, increasing confidence and self-esteem of learners and improving relationships amongst students and teachers.

Peer mentors and peer mentoring schemes seem to appear mainly in secondary schools where students moving up from Junior/Primary schools may need assistance in settling in to the whole new schedule and lifestyle of secondary school life. As part of their role a peer mentor can help their mentees with school work and study skills, but have also been used for wider issues, such as attendance, bullying issues, behavioural issues and for family problems that a learner may be experiencing.

Although peer mentoring as a term usually applies to learners mentoring learners there is also the opportunity for you to make use of cross-age peer mentoring. This is defined as:

> *An interpersonal relationship between different ages that reflects a greater degree of hierarchical power imbalance than is typical of a friendship and in which the goal is for the older to promote one or more aspects of the younger youth's development. It refers to a sustained (long-term), usually formalized (i.e. program-based), developmental relationship. The relationship is 'developmental' in that the older peer's goal is to help guide the younger mentee's development in domains such as interpersonal skills, self-esteem and conventional connectedness and attitudes.*

> *(DuBois and Karcher, 2005)*

Case study

Harvey has recently started a level 2 engineering apprenticeship with a local company and attends college one day a week on day release. His attendance in the workplace is excellent and his company are very pleased with the progress he has been making. However, his attendance at college is sporadic, and when he does attend he is often disruptive and difficult to deal with. The company is concerned that his lack of attendance and engagement with the college will create problems for him and he will not complete his apprenticeship successfully.

As a way of trying to encourage him to attend he was paired with a level 3 apprentice, who attended college the same day but was based in a different company. The pair worked together on the elements of the framework that was creating problems for Harvey and over a period of several weeks Harvey's attendance and engagement with class and tutors began to improve.

Consider the following:

1   What were the benefits in Harvey being paired with someone who was in a similar apprenticeship?
2   Would it have been appropriate for you to mentor him?
3   Would any of the other models of mentoring been an option for Harvey?
4   What other ways could you have supported him?

What is coaching?

Coaching targets high performance and improvement at work and usually focuses on specific skills and goals, although it may also have an impact on an individual's personal attributes (such as social interaction or confidence). The process typically lasts for a relatively short defined period of time, or forms the basis of ongoing personal development for an individual. For the teacher, the use of coaching techniques requires that the teacher refrains from their natural tendency to provide the learner with solutions to the problems she or he is facing. Rather, the teacher's role is to help the learner identify the problems and bring their own solutions to light. By asking the probing, open-ended questions, the teacher helps the learner to reflect and analyse a particular issue or problem and then asks the learner: 'What are you going to do about it?'

Employing this coaching strategy compels the learner to accept responsibility for his or her behaviour, or lack of progress.

Mentoring or coaching?

As a process, mentoring is quite often confused with coaching and the words used interchangeably. Maclennan (1995:4) defines coaching as:

> the process whereby one individual helps another; to unlock their natural ability; to perform, to learn, and achieve; to increase awareness of the factors that determine performance; to increase their sense of self-responsibility and ownership of their performance; to self-coach to identify and remove barriers to achievement.

There are several coaching techniques available to you as a teacher. The Hersey and Blanchard model of coaching categorises learners from 1–4 as shown below.

D1 – Low competence, high commitment – in general these learners are lacking the specific skills and techniques they need to achieve, but are committed and have the confidence and/or motivation to want to succeed.

D2 – Some competence, low commitment – these learners have some experience, but still need support. Their confidence may have fallen following a specific task or piece or work. They may be wondering if they are capable of achieving. These learners could also be classed as being in a negative syndrome (Hohman, 2008) with low levels of ability and low levels of motivation.

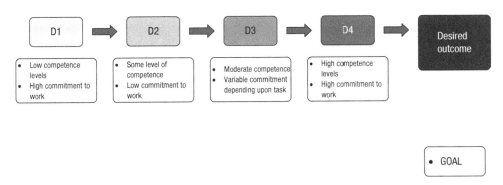

FIGURE 7.3 Models of coaching

Adapted from Hershey and Blanchard (Senior, 2010)

D3 – Moderate competence, variable commitment – these learners are relatively experienced and competent with the subject and subject knowledge, but may lack confidence to work without the support of the coach, or they may lack the motivation.

D4 – High competence, high commitment – learners who are experienced and confident in their ability. They are in a positive syndrome, being highly motivated and very capable of succeeding.

As the coach to this diverse range of learners you have several different approaches available to you to support their learning, and how you approach the coaching role will depend upon the types of learners that you have in your classroom. For the D1 learner you may wish to consider incentivising them, and allowing them to make their own choices, but still challenging and guiding them if they go of task. For the D2 learner you will need to be much more directive in your approach to their learning. D3 requires an encouraging approach, and D4 more of a facilitator role.

According to Senior (2010), no matter which of the skills and quadrants you find yourself working in with a learner it is important to remember the following:

- **For the person being mentored**, the quickest way to succeed is to learn from, and to model people who have made a success of their lives. This could be you, or a famous chef, television presenter, pop star or many others depending upon the subject area that the learner is studying.

- **For the mentor**, the opportunity for self-reflection about their own career path together with an increased understanding of their discipline and its development is a major benefit for a teacher.

TABLE 7.2 Four quadrants of coaching

S2 – Guiding – two-way communication; the learner still needs direction, as they lack experience and some commitment. The teacher allows the learner to make choices and decisions, but will challenge if the learners is going off track. To be used with D2 learners.	**S4 – Delegating** – the coach needs to give little direction or support. This is for learners who have high competence and high confidence/motivation level. The learner decides when the coach needs to be involved. To be used with D4 learners.
S1 – Directing – coach (teacher) focuses on giving direction, telling the learner what they need to do and making sure they do it. To be used with D1 learners.	**S3 – Supporting** – less direction needed, but still offering a lot of support. The learners are now making their own decisions. They need less direction because they have the necessary skills, but still need a coach to boost their confidence and/or motivation level. To be used with D3 learners.

The differences between coaching and mentoring in the classroom

As previously discussed, the terms mentoring and coaching are sometime used interchangeably, and whilst both roles can employ similar techniques there are differences in the way in which they are used in the classroom.

In taking on the role of a mentor with a learner your main focus will be on the individual and their needs at any particular point in time; with a coach the focus is almost always on an individual's performance. With a mentoring role the teacher takes on the role of a facilitator and mentor meetings do not normally have set agendas but are based upon a relationship of mutual trust, whereas a coach is more likely to have a specific agenda that has been set with the coachee.

Ethical considerations of mentoring in the classroom

As a concept, ethics involves the use of reasoned moral judgments to examine one's responsibility in any given situation. Mentors have the responsibility of teaching and role-modelling the appropriate ethical behavior of academic professionals. Both mentors and mentees have the responsibility of behaving ethically in their relationship, and regardless of the role that you choose to adopt with your learners there is a note of caution regarding the ethics surrounding the tutoring, mentoring process.

What elements are associated with appropriate ethical behavior in the mentee/mentor relationship?

As a tutor, teacher, trainer or employer there are several areas where your ethical conduct is important within the mentor/mentee relationship.

The following areas are some that you may wish to consider:

- Maintaining confidentiality – as a tutor and mentor there will be certain discussions that need to remain confidential between you and the learner. However, you also need to be aware of when to involve others, or when to signpost the learner to other areas. For example, if a learner discloses abuse or talks about suicide you need to refer them to professional counsellors, student services or guidance personnel. Further information on ethics and confidentiality can be found in the suggested reading at the end of the chapter.

- Professionalism – perhaps the most obvious professional roles within mentoring are the roles in which you are currently working – teacher, lecturer or tutor. However, within your setting there are also other professionals with whom your learners may have contact. For example, administrative staff or classroom assistants. The most important thing to remember under the ethical consideration of professionalism is that whilst recognising that there are no real clear demarcation lines you will need an understanding of boundaries. Gabriel (2000) defines these boundaries as complex, with the main issues surrounding relationship boundaries. Your setting may have guidelines to follow here.

- Equal opportunities – we have all been in a situation where we have had a learner who has been very demanding, requiring constant attention and support. We need to ensure that when mentoring our learners we allow equal access to all and that within that access each individual has equal opportunity and support to that of their peers.

- College or schools policy and practice – this section would be incomplete without mentioning the need to be aware of your college or school policy at all times. What are the guidelines for meeting learners, is it within the normal working day? Can you meet them at the end of the working day? If you are a male teacher working with female learners, what are the regulations surrounding one-one meetings?

- Promoting mutual respect and trust.

- Being diligent in providing knowledge, wisdom, and developmental support.

- Maintaining vigilance with regard to the mentee/mentor relationship (superior power increases the mentor's obligation to be cognizant of the mentee's feelings and rights).

- Acknowledging skills and experiences that each bring to the mentee/mentor relationship.

- Carefully framing advice and feedback.

Activity

Colin is a fairly confident, outgoing student who has just completed his first year of a hospitality qualification. He has excelled at his practical work but struggles with some of the more academic work, in particular his functional maths classes. As the programme manager for the hospitality course you have been asked by his tutor to try and support him with this.

1   What style of mentoring or coaching do you think would be appropriate to try with him?
2   What personal skills would you need to support him effectively?

Benefits of mentoring

If taken seriously by the learner the mentoring process can focus and motivate them towards achieving their learning goals and develop them as individuals.

For the mentee

In today's complex and often highly competitive world of vocational education, having a mentor, either classroom or work-based, can mean the difference between success and failure and can help the learner to develop and progress in their chosen career. A mentor can answer questions as they arise for the mentee and thereby ensure steady progress and completion of course milestones, whether that be assignment work, work with functional skills or just general careers advice. The interest and the support of a mentor often provide the mentee with confidence to undertake a new and exciting challenge.

For the mentor

Mentoring provides the mentor with numerous benefits, including enhancement of his or her own personal and professional knowledge while teaching and learning from the mentee. By providing guidance, support, advice, strategic feedback, and other insights to a mentee, the mentor can learn and enhance leadership skills. Mentees often bring a fresh perspective to a difficult problem, and serving as a mentor can provide a renewed sense of purpose. Most importantly, being a mentor can give you as a teacher a sense of satisfaction in contributing to a legacy of developing the next generation of skilled workers.

Reflecting on practice

Reflect back to when you were a student in secondary school, college or university. Are there any relationships that you now recognise as being an informal mentoring relationship? What benefits have you taken and retained from that relationship?

Conclusion

In summary, coaching and mentoring can be very powerful tools to support you with your 14–19 learners. As a teacher, trainer, tutor or employer you will need to be aware of your learners and their needs before making a decision on the type and appropriateness of mentoring as a process to support them in their learning. At all times you need to remember that every learner is unique and whatever approach you decide upon you will need to be flexible as your learners grow and develop their skills and confidence.

References

Clutterbuck, D. (1985) *Consenting Adults Making the Most of Mentoring*. London: Channel Four Television.

Darwin, A. (2004) 'Characteristics Ascribed to Mentors by their Protégés'. in Clutterbuck & Lane (eds) *The Situational Mentor: An International Review of Competences and Capabilities in Mentoring*. Farnham: Gower Publishing Ltd.

DuBois, David L., & Karcher, Michael J. (2005). *Handbook of Youth Mentoring*. Thousand Oaks, California: SAGE Publications Ltd.

Gabriel, Y. (2000) *Storytelling in Organizations: Fact, Fictions and Fantasies*. Oxford: Oxford University Press.

Hohman, D. (2008) cited in *The International Journal of Mentoring and Coaching*, VI(2).

Maclennan, N. (1995) *Coaching and Mentoring*. Abingdon: Routledge.

Pollard, A., Purvis, J. & Walford, G. (1997) *Education and Training and the New Vocationalism*. Buckingham: Open University Press.

Senior, L. (2010) *The Essential Guide to Teaching 14–19 Diplomas*. London: Pearson.

Rhodes, J.E., Grossman, J.B., & Resch, N.R. (2000). 'Agents of change: Pathways through which mentoring relationships influence adolescents' academic adjustment', *Child Development*, 71: 1662–1671.

Further reading

Clutterbuck, D., & Lane, G. (eds) (2004) *The Situational Mentor: An International Review of Competences and Capabilities in Mentoring*. Farnham: Gower Publishing Ltd.

Whitmore J. (2002) *Coaching For Performance: Growing People, Performance and Purpose*. London: Brearley.

Reflective practice 14–19

After studying this chapter you will be able to:

- define reflective practice;
- identify models of reflective practice;
- discuss the reflective practice process;
- consider how effective reflection can help learning in the classroom.

Introduction

In addition to having a good working knowledge of the learning, teaching and assessment strategies that are available to a teacher working within 14–19, it is also important to be able to draw upon other skills to ensure that your learner is progressing and achieving as he or she should. This chapter explores the use of reflective practice for you as the teacher and how it can help your practice, and explores the areas of reflection and reflective practice as strategies to use in the classroom to encourage your learners.

What is reflective practice?

'A reflection in a mirror is an exact replica of what is in front of it. Reflection in practice, however, gives back not what it is, but what it might be, an improvement on the original'.

(Biggs, 1999:6)

The concept of reflective practice is now widely employed in the field of teacher education and teacher professional development and is the basis for many programmes of initial teacher education. In education, reflective practice refers to the process of the educator studying his or her own teaching methods and determining what works best for the students. In simple terms reflection is about thinking about what has just happened, or is happening at any given point in time. Scales

(2013: 20) believes that refection is the 'one quality above all others that makes a good teacher'. In the classroom the ability to reflect allows us to adapt and change our practice to ensure that we are continually developing as teachers.

Moon defines reflective practice as 'a set of abilities and skills, to indicate the taking of a critical stance, an orientation to problem solving or state of mind' (1999: 63). The Higher Education Academy defines it as 'an approach that promotes autonomous learning that aims to develop students' understanding and critical thinking skills' (www.heacademy.ac.uk/enhancement/definitions/ reflective-practice accessed 20 July, 2015). Reflective practice can take several different approaches, the first being reflection on a particular situation in terms of what happened, who did what, and how you felt about it (common-sense reflecting). The second approach takes common-sense reflection one step further, through learning from the reflection to improving and developing (reflective thinking). A third approach is reflection in action and reflection on action (reflective practice). Reflection in action is reflection that takes place during a particular activity and reflection on action is the reflection completed at the end of a particular activity (Schon, 1983).

Reflective practice can be an important tool in practice-based professional learning settings where people learn from their own professional experiences, rather than from formal learning or knowledge transfer. The process can help us monitor our own development and competency within any given task.

Theories of reflection

I have already mentioned Moon as one of the theorists of reflection and reflective practice. There are several other theorists that should be considered when examining reflective practice.

Reflective practice can be said to date back to Socrates, Plato or Aristotle, but more recently, one of the most influential theorists was John Dewey, who in 1933 had discussed the concept of 'routine action' and 'reflective action'. The former being the day-to-day events within working life and the latter the engagement with self- appraisal and personal development.

Schon

Schon (1983) developed the concept of reflection in action and reflection on action. Again, in simple terms this means reflecting during an activity and reflecting after an activity. As a teacher one of the most important things you will learn is to reflect in action. Many new and beginning teachers find this very difficult to do, and they stick rigidly to the lesson plan, timings and activities that they have prepared. However, as a teacher you need to be constantly aware and monitoring the session as it develops. This awareness and monitoring then enables you to make changes if the situation requires it.

Activity: reflecting in action

Sarah is a beginning teacher, and has planned a one-hour session on the principles of marketing for her business studies group. After 15 minutes of explaining the four P's (product, price, place and promotion) she becomes aware that many of her learners are distracted and not listening to what she is saying.

What should she do to bring things back on track?

For Sarah there were several options. She could have considered her delivery method – was it too much talk and did she need to look at other methods? Could she have introduced some group activity to look at the four Ps and break things up?

Reflecting in action is about 'thinking on your feet', it can be second nature to the more experienced teacher but more scary for the newer teacher.

Kolb and Gibbs

The concept that reflection as an activity links theory and practice is attributed to Kolb and Gibb and their iterative models of reflective practice and learning cycle. Kolb's model (1976) is based on experiential learning and relies on the teacher planning, doing, reviewing and drawing conclusions before repeating the cycle. This model not only questions the 'what' within an event but expands this by asking 'why' to evaluate and analyse the event.

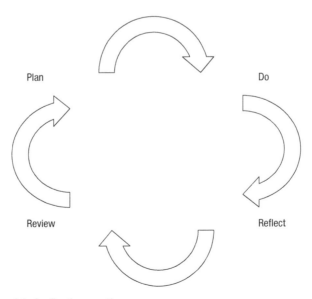

Plan

Do

Review

Reflect

FIGURE 8.1 Kolb's model of reflective practice

Adapted from Kolb, 1976

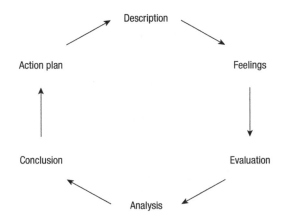

FIGURE 8.2 Gibb's reflective cycle

Adapted from Gibb, 1988

Consider a teacher using group work as part of a planned session. The group work does not go to plan and the learners find it difficult to complete the task. Following the session, using Kolb's model the teacher would talk to more experienced colleagues and complete some research into what makes good group work activities. The next session he or she would then use the new knowledge to incorporate the new activity into the planning.

Gibbs' model (1988) is a six stage model based upon learning by doing.

This model makes the process of reflective practice more complete through the explicit need for the reflective process to include action plans that will inform future learning. In unpacking this process Gibbs provides a series of questions that can be used with the learner:

- Description: 'What happened?

- Feelings: What was your reaction, how did you feel about this?

- Evaluation: Was what happened positive or negative for you?

- Conclusion: What conclusions can you draw about you as a teacher or the situation?

- Action plan: What will you do next time, will things be different?

Brookfield

Brookfield (1998) proposed that reflective practitioners constantly reflect on their practice through four complementary lenses: the lens of their autobiography (or self) as learners of reflective practice, the lens of other learners' eyes, the lens of colleagues' experiences, and the lens of theoretical, philosophical and research literature; and that these four lenses will reflect back to us starkly different pictures of who we are and what we do.

Lens 1 – autobiography or self

Teachers may focus on their experiences as a teacher in order to reveal aspects of their pedagogy that may need adjustment or strengthening. Self-reflection is at the heart of reflective practice and often involves an individual engagement with results, suggestions, comments and evidence obtained through the other lenses.

Lens 2 – other learners

Engaging with student views of the learning environment can lead to more responsive teaching. Evaluations, assessments, journals, focus groups and/or interviews can each provide cues to improve teaching and learning. Gathering feedback from students can provide valuable insight into teaching and learning. For Brookfield, when teachers reflect on their practice using the student lens they become more responsive to the needs of students. Student-centered teaching is vitally important in helping students gain the most out of their education.

Lens 3 – colleagues and peers

Peers can highlight hidden habits in teaching practice, and also provide innovative solutions to teaching problems. Further, colleagues can be inspirational and provide support and solidarity. Teaching practice can benefit greatly from the involvement of peers in the observation and review of teaching and learning. There are many ways in which teachers can learn from feedback provided by their peers, and observing the teaching of others can enhance reflection on one's own teaching. Peers might observe your teaching, review your class plans or course outlines, mentor you through promotion or award processes, or help you interpret feedback and plan any alterations to your teaching. Fellow teachers can provide helpful observations and advice, and the process of peer reflection can create supportive teaching environments, help overcome academic isolation and lead to confident, reflective teachers.

Lens 4 – theory

Teaching theory provides the vocabulary for teaching practice, and offers different ways to view and understand your teaching. There are numerous benefits for teachers who engage with the literature of teaching and learning. For example, you may discover ideas for overcoming teaching struggles, new feedback strategies or interpretive techniques, a strong vocabulary to express teaching beliefs, and/or wider social, political and cultural contexts for your teaching.

Activity: using Brookfield

Consider the four lenses identified by Brookfield as a means of reflection. How might you as a teacher use each of these lenses? Identify one activity that would be appropriate. Can Brookfield be applied to your 14–19 learners? What activities would you use for them?

Why reflect as teachers?

As a teacher there are several reasons for reflection, not least how could you improve or change and develop classroom practice.

Roffey-Barentsen and Malthouse (2009) identify ten benefits of reflective practice for the teacher.

- Improvement of teaching – if you take the time to reflect on what you have planned and delivered in the classroom you can identify what went well and what areas you need to improve, then your overall teaching should improve.

- Learning from reflection – if you use reflection effectively you will learn from the process. This may be something as simple as reading up on a topic or speaking to colleagues about how to deal with particular behaviours.

- Enhancing problem solving skills – reflection will always raise some questions for you as the teacher. By analysing these questions you will come to a solution and in doing so improve your problem-solving skills.

- Enabling critical thinking – effective reflection enables you to become more critical in your self-evaluation and lead to more effective decision making.

- Enabling decision making – as you reflect on your practice, you will find you need to make decisions about what to do (or not to do) next. You may well have a number of choices which you have to weigh up, and deciding which one to take can be difficult. If you regularly reflect on your teaching in depth, you are regularly going to come across the need to make decisions, but the results of your reflective practice will help you to make those decisions in a more informed, thoughtful and objective manner.

- Improving organisational skills – If you are thinking carefully about what you are doing, identifying possible actions and choices, trying out solutions, and adjusting what you do to take account of the results, this involves a good deal of organisation. By breaking down issues and problems into steps or stages, you will get better at organising your time and your activity to concentrate on the important, 'solution-focused' actions.

- Managing personal change – reflection can affect how you perceive yourself and your abilities. Effective reflection can enable you to make personal change in your circumstances or situation.

- Acknowledging personal values – reflective practice can be used to acknowledge that your own values may sometimes differ from colleagues or the external environment and can help you to choose approaches and actions which can help you to resolve those clashes without it adversely affecting the professional balance of your work as a teacher.

- Listening and taking self-advice – we all tend to be self-critical, effective reflection can remove that self-critique so that we become less averse to negativity, and more open to the fact things may not be as we had hoped.

- Recognising emancipatory benefits – having control over your own teaching.

Reflective practice is not however just something that we should do as teachers. If used correctly within the classroom, reflective practice can benefit the learner, their progress and learning, whether that be in the completion of a particular task or activity, or the way they work in group situations.

Reflection for the learner

Activity

Reflection will enable the learner to consider the most appropriate way in which to approach a task or activity. Many learners will go through the problem-solving process without realising that they have done so, although some learners may need prompting. When you next give your group an activity or tasks to complete, give them a prompt sheet to work through before they actually start the task. The prompt sheet should allow them to consider four questions:

- What is the task? (clarification);
- What are the possible issues/problems? (analysis);
- What could I do? (deliberation);
- What shall I do? (selection).

Following the completion of the task the learner should then be encouraged to consider the final question:

- Did it work? (evaluation).

For the learner the benefits of critical thinking and decision making appear to be synonymous with problem solving, in that decision making is part of the problem-solving process. Our learners will have to make a decision as to which of the possible options available to them should be used. The critical-thinking element comes in when the learners are able to make informed judgments, based on all of the available information, rejecting information that is incomplete, incorrect or not appropriate. Not all of our learners will be adept at critical thinking.

However, reflection can help improve this skill by allowing the learner the time to consider, analyse and then make decisions. If we consider some of the benefits identified above for the teacher in reflection we can see how these can also be applied to the learner.

Organisational skills

Organisational skills tend to be skills that many young people have difficulty with as prioritising their personal lives above that of school or college is often more tempting. However, in the 14–19 curriculum, effective learning will require the learner to have some degree of organisational and self-management skills to complete their tasks. Whether that be within a classroom-based setting or out in the workplace.

Managing personal change, acknowledging personal values and listening and taking self-advice

These areas are skills and attributes that a learner may find most difficult to reconcile, as managing personal change relies on a learner being able to look inward and analyse their own thoughts and feelings whilst being aware of others around them. This form of reflection can sometimes lead to negativity, with the learner becoming convinced that they are inadequate and incapable of completing the tasks set. Other learners may react differently, and rather than believing themselves inadequate, believe it is the fault of the teacher that they cannot complete the task – they haven't been taught well, the teacher was rubbish, it's a waste of time, are things that you may hear in your classroom. The art of self-reflection is to encourage the learner to change their perceptions and in so doing change their attitudes towards the tasks in hand, taking advice from both their inner self and from others, whilst acknowledging that everyone has a right to their own opinions. Harris (1986) sums this acknowledgement up in the following diagram.

The quadrant to strive for is 'I'm OK. You're OK', as here the learner accepts both his or her own values and those of others equally. 'I'm OK. You're not OK' indicates that the learner thinks that they are right and everyone else is wrong. 'I'm not OK. You're OK' indicates that the learner is insecure and looks to others for support and guidance regardless of their own feelings, and the final box, 'I'm not OK. You're not OK' indicates a situation where a learner sees both themselves and others as worthless.

TABLE 8.1 The art of self-reflection

I'm OK	I'm OK
You're OK	You're not OK
I'm not OK	I'm not OK
You're OK	You're not OK

Adapted from Harris 1986

The reflective practice process as a learning tool

Hatton and Smith (1995) identified four essential issues concerning reflection:

- We should learn to frame and reframe complex or ambiguous problems, test out various interpretations, and then modify our actions consequently.
- Our thoughts should be extended and systematic by looking back upon our actions some time after they have taken place.
- Certain activities labelled as reflective, such as the use of journals or group discussions following practical experiences, are often not directed towards the solution of specific problems.
- We should consciously account for the wider historic, cultural, and political values or beliefs in framing practical problems to arrive at a solution. This is often identified as critical reflection. However, the term critical reflection, like reflection itself, appears to be used loosely, some taking it to mean no more than constructive self-criticism of one's actions with a view to improvement.

If you look back at the chapter on learning and teaching and the various learning styles and learning types you will recall the reflective learner as being an identified typology. This typology believes that reflective learners gain understanding most thoroughly and efficiently when they are allowed the freedom to take time to reflect on the information and instruction they have been given. Reflective learners are typically intrapersonal, logical, mathematical learners with a tendency toward a thinker personality type. It is suggested that reflective learners should:

- study in a quiet environment free from any distractions;
- when reading, take several breaks to think about and reflect on what they have read, to help them comprehend and retain the subject matter more efficiently;
- try to avoid merely memorising the subject matter by answer the questions Who? What? Where? When? Why? and How?
- Summarise the subject matter, and apply it to their world.
                    (Learning Assessment Survey, Texas Tech University)

I would argue that all learners need to be reflective, whether that is a natural preference or not, and that we as reflective teachers can provide the scaffold and support to encourage reflection, even in those where it does not come naturally. The natural reflective learner will automatically absorb, rather than act on new information. They will think through an idea and its ramifications, and often enjoy working independently, at least before doing a group activity. Note that reflective learners are not passive learners in the sense that they only want to receive information. On the contrary, they wish to cognitively process and reason with educator input so that it conforms to their particular intellectual framework. The active learner on the other hand is more likely to jump straight in! So what can you do as a 14–19 teacher to encourage better reflection?

Hatton and Smith (1995) suggested four possible activities that may aid reflection in the classroom:

- action research projects;
- case and cultural studies;
- practical experiences;
- structured curriculum tasks:
  - reading fiction and non-fiction;
  - oral interviews;
  - writing tasks, such as narratives, biographies, reflective essays and keeping journals.

However, although these strategies have the potential to encourage reflection, there is little research evidence to show that this is actually being achieved.

Extending evaluative feedback might have even more powerful effects. Providing probes may cause the learner to continue to think about the topic, such as:

- 'Have you thought about how a skilled operator might do this?'
- 'But how much does safety really get compromised when you don't use safety shoes?'

Pointing out other possibilities may also result in additional thinking about relationships among factors not previously considered, such as:

- 'Another factor you might consider is how many different tools will be required if you use different sized bolts in the design?'
- 'But what if the rate of water flow is doubled?'

Although such feedback may be provided via written comments, they are probably most powerful when used interactively in interpersonal dialogue. Carrying on a dialogue with one or more learners about the work they have submitted is probably the ultimate in promoting reflection via feedback. But the logistics of doing so and having discussion leaders who are skilled in the content and possess good interpersonal skills may be beyond the capacity of the system to provide; unless it is computer-mediated in some way.

Other hints for encouraging reflection include:

- Seek alternatives.
- View from various perspectives.
- Seek the framework, theoretical basis, underlying rationale (of behaviours, methods, techniques, programmes).

- Compare and contrast.
- Put into different/varied contexts.
- Ask 'what if . . .?'
- Consider consequences.

Activity

As teachers we need to know our learners and their strengths and weakness so that we can support their development. How would you encourage your learner to explore their feelings and experiences? You may wish to look at the chapter on social and emotional development to help you better understand the 14–19 year old and their approach to the classroom.

Through reflection our learners will challenge their assumptions, ask new questions and try to make sense of their experiences. Instead of being passive receivers of external expert knowledge, they then become active creators (and co-creators) of knowledge.

The figure below demonstrates how increased reflection encourages increased learning.

Again, in simple terms this model suggests that a learner will move through the various stages of reflection, firstly taking notice of a particular event or situation. They will then move to a situation whereby they try to make sense and create meaning around the event. This in turn leads to a learner making decisions based on their understanding and moving to a level of transformation in how they learn and progress.

Reflective journals for the 14–19 learner (or teacher)

A reflective journal is a personal expression of experiences and feelings, therefore there is no right or wrong way for a learner (or teacher) to develop their own. Everyone has different qualities that make him or her unique and a journal should and could take many different forms that reflect the uniqueness of that individual. A journal can be electronic, a sketchbook, a notebook, a binder, an audiotape or a

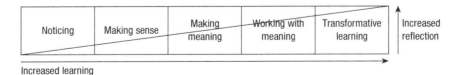

FIGURE 8.3 Increased reflection and increased learning

Adapted from Moon, 2004

combination of some or all of these forms. A 'record' in it can include such things as written reflections, drawings, doodles, pictures, poems, colours, clippings, quotes, descriptions of dreams, double-entry journaling and mind mapping or branching. The benefits of each of the different forms or styles are for the end user – you or your learner.

Reflective writing, or reflective journals, are made up of several elements:

- personal descriptive account of the experience or situation;
- your feelings about the situation;
- an evaluation of what worked, what went well and what did not go well;
- an evaluation of what you would change, add or remove for the next time.

It is important that the reflection belongs to the learner, in that way they will engage more fully with the process and eventually reflection will become a regular habit.

What are the challenges associated with reflective practice for you and your learner?

Reflective practice as a process can be quite challenging for some learners and teachers, especially if not incorporated or embedded into the learning itself. Some people get hung up on what they should write and indeed why they should write things, especially when they are asked to link their reflections to theory as is the case with some teacher education programmes. The best form of reflection is narrative – simply what happened – what were the consequences and what should be done differently? Some of the key challenges, and/or excuses around reflection are detailed below.

Time

When your time is pressured, which is common as a teacher or a learner with deadlines to meet, reflection is often something that can be cut from process – why should you take additional time to reflect when the task is more important? Although difficult to reconcile, people work both more effectively and efficiently if they use reflective practice, as they make more clear and informed decisions, are more aware of what is likely to work and what is not, and are more up to date with what works elsewhere.

Emotions

Reflecting carefully on what you do can be challenging and quite scary, and for the 14–19 learner may be something that creates confidence issues. As a teacher you may come to some conclusions which have major consequences for you as a professional, especially if you have doubts about yourself as a person and as a professional, as these can appear at times to be reinforced by reflection.

Not being naturally reflective

You may well be someone who doesn't tend to find reflection something you naturally get involved in – you may well be a 'doer' rather than a 'thinker'. This may be the case with your students as well.

Conclusion

Reflection is a practice that facilitates the exploration, examination and understanding of what we are feeling, thinking and learning. It is a thoughtful consideration of academic material, personal experiences and interpersonal relationships. Reflection is a form of internal inquiry that extends the relevance of theory and deepens our understanding of the practice of our everyday life and work.

Reflection and reflective practice is a key process for both learners and teachers and is a way in which we can create meaning and therefore a better understanding of why and how things work. As a concept it enables us to step back from the situation and think about the next steps and what actions we should take. Reflective practice can help our learners put their learning into context by encouraging them to make links between the classroom and the real-life situation. It can be used as a method of self-improvement, enabling learners to consider their performances both from an academic perspective and also a personal perspective. It is also important to note that the art of reflection may not come easily to some learners and that at some stage in your career as a 14–19 teacher you will find yourself in the role of mentor or coach to help your learners succeed.

References

Biggs, J. (1999) *Teaching for Quality Learning at University.* Buckingham: Open University Press.

Brookfield, S. (1988) 'Developing Critically Reflective Practitioners: A Rationale for Training Educators of Adults' in Brookfield, S. (ed), *Training Educators of Adults: The Theory and Practice of Graduate Adult Education.* New York: Routledge.

Gibbs, G. (1988) *Learning by Doing.* London, Further Education Unit.

Harris, T. A. & Harris, A. B. (1986) *Staying OK.* London: Pan Books

Hatton, N. & Smith, D. (1995) *Reflection in Teacher Education: Towards Definition and Implementation.* Sydney: The University of Sydney School of Teaching and Curriculum Studies (www: http://www2.edfac.usyd.edu.au/LocalResource/Study1/hattonart.html)

Klasen, N. & Clutterbuck, D. (2001) *Implementing Mentoring Schemes.* London: Routledge.

Kolb, D. A. (1976). *Experiential Learning: Experience As the Source of learning and Development*. New Jersey: Prentice Hall.

Moon, J. (1999) *Learning Journals: A Handbook for Academics, Students and Professional Development*. London: Kogan Page.

Roffey-Barentsen, J. & Malthouse, R. (2009) *Reflective Practice in the Lifelong Learning Sector*. Exeter: Learning Matters.

Scales, P. (2013). *Teaching in the Lifelong Learning Sector* (2nd edition). London: Open University Press.

Schon, D.A. (1983) *The Reflective Practitioner*. New York: Basic Books.

Texas Tech University. *Learning Assessment Survey*. (Online. Available at: http://www.pssc.ttu.edu/techhort/lasrvy/a_r.htm)

Further reading

Aldridge, S. & Rigby, S. (eds) (2006) *Counselling Skills in Context*. Abingdon: Hodder and Stoughton.

Biggs, J. & Collins, K. (1982) *Evaluating the Quality of Learning: The SOLO Taxonomy*. New York: Academic Press.

Bolton, G. (2005) *Reflective Practice: Writing and Professional Development*. London: Sage.

Dewey, J. (1933) *How We Think: A Restatement of the Relation of Reflective Thinking to the Educative Process*. Boston: D.C. Heath.

Green, M. (2001) *Successful Tutoring: Good Practice for Managers and Tutors*. London: LSDA

Greenaway, R. (2002) *Experiential Learning Cycles*. www.reviewing.co.uk/research/learning.cycles.htm

Maclennan, N. (1995) *Coaching and Mentoring*. Aldershot:, Gower Publishing.

Mayes, A. (ed) *Early Professional Development for Teachers*. London: David Fulton.

Moon, J. (2004) *A Handbook of Reflective and Experiential Learning Theory and Practice*. Abingdon: Routledge

Rollett, B.A. (2001) 'How do expert teachers view themselves?', in F. Banks & A. Shelton-Mayes (eds) *Early Professional Development for Teachers*. London: David Fulton.

Wider skills for the 14–19 practitioner

Teacher knowledge and CPD

As a concept, CPD for the 14–19 sector has experienced rapid growth in both interest and uptake over the last few years. This can be partially attributed to the introduction of a dual professionalism CPD model for teachers in the lifelong learning sector (normally, but not exclusively, post-compulsory education and training). This model was introduced by the Institute for Learning (IfL) in 2007, who were at the time the professional body for the lifelong learning sector. This dual model suggested that CPD for practitioners could be structured and organised in a number of different ways, and taken up for a number of different reasons. The IfL's model identifies the dual professional aspects of teaching, namely a combination of subject specialism and teaching and learning set within the work context. Their CPD model also suggests various topics that may be identified as CPD activities.

However, it can be questioned whether the concept of CPD is appropriate and specific enough to enable the 14–19 practitioner and workforce to create appropriate knowledge for the 14–19 practitioner, and I would suggest from the model proposed by the IfL that the teacher takes ownership of his or her training, which is one characteristic identified by Peel (2005) as being integral to professionalism.

As a vocational 14–19 model the following figure shows the components that are important to have knowledge of when teaching 14–19.

However, much CPD is directed towards achieving institutional targets determined by external authorities, and as a consequence teachers' perceptions of ownership are diminished or perceived as of little value or significance as no

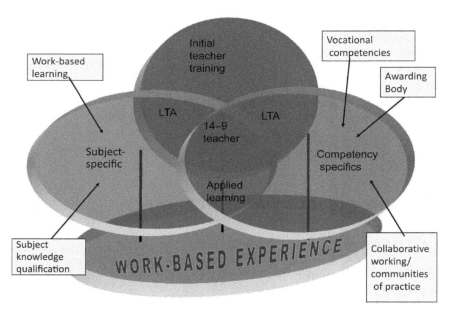

FIGURE 9.1 Professionalism

Senior: 2015 based on IfL 2007

recognition is placed on their personal professional needs (Eaton and Carbonne, 2008). Hargreaves (1998) argues that the traditional model of CPD does not take into account the teacher's needs and that a practising teacher should be more involved in the process of creating CPD requirements.

Patrick, Ford and Mcphee (2003) acknowledge that CPD is viewed as an extension of initial teacher training, based upon competencies and giving rise to continued professional registration, whilst Hegarty (2000) challenged the notion of CPD being based upon competency, noting that over-reliance on competency can lead to impoverished teaching, lacking insight and creativity.

Grangeat and Gray (2007) develop this notion of professional competency in their discussion of two models of professional competency development and their use in developing innovative vocational curricula and CPD. These two models – the *didactique professionelle* (DP) model, and the 'work process knowledge' (WPK) model – have both emerged from the 'new industrial landscape'. Within this landscape the DP model was originally developed to study processes of professional efficiency enhancement (Boreham et al., 2002), whereas the WPK model was designed to demonstrate competency in an arena whereby work processes had changed (Pastré, 2004). These two models have been discussed in relation to education, with some researchers believing that education involves both types of professional competency, and that this is a new and emerging trend in education – that teachers do not only provide knowledge, but also encourage learning through the generation of activity (Grangeat, 2004; McNally et al., 2004; Robert and Rogalski, 2005). This suggests that transmission of knowledge is not enough and that education needs to enable young people to apply their knowledge to particular experiences.

Boreham (2002) furthers this discussion by arguing that professional knowledge enhancement arises from efforts to resolve differences between theoretical knowledge, what the standard operating procedure tells teachers to do and what confronts them in reality. Samurçay and Vidal-Gomel (2002) discuss an example of electrical work to highlight that the model includes both standard electrical theory and previous personal experiences. Boreham (2004) notes that three types of knowledge are required for effectiveness: (1) personal professional experiences (of other agents, partners, users, machines, artefacts and previous problems); (2) all the resources and artefacts that exist in the work situation (procedure manuals, ICT, etc.); (3) theoretical knowledge from vocational curricula.

However, while an increasing range of literature focuses on particular aspects of CPD, there is a paucity of literature addressing the spectrum of CPD models in a comparative manner (Hoban, 2002).

Kennedy (2005) identified nine models of CPD and the knowledge areas attached to each one: training; award-bearing; deficit; cascade; standards-based; coaching/mentoring; community of practice; action research; transformative. I would argue that the CPD framework suggested by the IfL is that of a deficit model suggested by Kennedy (2005), designed for organisations or individuals to determine areas of weakness within the performance of the individual teacher. The framework attempts to remedy these weaknesses by identifying the areas of under-performance. However, Kennedy (2005) suggests that the expected level of effectiveness is unclear, so that in reality the model views CPD as a 'means of remedying individual weaknesses, whereby collective responsibility is not considered' (Kennedy,2005: 239). Rhodes and Beneicke (2003) develop this notion further through the suggestion that poor teaching performance can also be attributed to organisational and management practices and the educational system itself.

It could then be suggested that the idea of CPD is integral to the development of the teacher and not something developed from the three specific areas as suggested by the model above.

For the 14–19 teacher, the entry point will vary from a new entrant to the profession to an existing qualified teacher, and may even take into account the practitioner who provides specialist input to the programme, whilst still remaining in the workplace. It is also important to note that within the 14–19 arena the system and management practices also ought to be taken into account when designing effective CPD.

If we consider the standards-based model of CPD identified by Kennedy it could be argued that as a dual profession, 14–19 teaching lends itself to a standards base. In particular, the introduction of a standards-based vocational curriculum would suggest that this model would be effective in ensuring that the teacher was competent in the areas needed to teach the 14–19 student. Building on the DP model of Grangreat and Gray (2007), it is my belief that the arena of CPD is linked to the workplace, which in the case of vocational education is not just the teaching arena, but also the location in which the subject is situated. If, therefore, this model is concerned with professional efficiency enhancement, then any CPD needs to take into account both subject and generic pedagogy, with an emphasis on application of subject to the practice, coupled with external accountability. However, as early as 1991, Smyth (1991) argued that externally imposed accountability indicated a lack of respect for the teachers' own professional learning and reflective enquiry. Beyer (2002) added to this argument by suggesting that the standards-based model of CPD within teacher education narrows the range of activities to focus on account-ability and external scrutiny, whilst Adams and Hambright (2005) posited that to be effective, CPD is a result of the initiative of the teacher themselves and based upon their own motivations.

So what should be the way forward for CPD within the 14–19 arena? I would suggest that a transformative model as identified by Kennedy (2005) would appear to be the most appropriate model, as it has at its heart a number of pro-cesses taken from the other models of CPD and recognises a range of different conditions and situations within which CPD will occur. Hoban (2002) suggests that this model supports educational change and that what is needed for the sec-tor is not a context-specific model, as suggested by the IfL, but rather a balance between the different stakeholders within the sector and an integration of the range of models available in a short and individual approach.

Kennedy (2005) also suggests that when designing a CPD model a set of ques-tions should be asked to identify the model most appropriate for those involved in its implementation. She suggested that the first question should regard the types of knowledge needed, procedural or propositional. The second should be whether the focus lies with collective or individual development. The third and fourth questions are based around professional autonomy and accountability, whilst the final questions relate to the perceived purposes of the CPD (Kennedy 2005). These final questions also link to work by Villegas-Reimers and Reimers (2000) who suggested that CPD models can be used to either provide people with the skills needed to do what is required of them (usually by a third party) or to inform and contribute to development. Kennedy further purported that these two areas are distinct and therefore need different models of CPD. Evans (2002) also supported the concept that any CPD should be based around individual needs and believed that the attitudinal element of development is dependent upon the teacher recognising that his or her practice is unsatisfactory.

New approaches to continuing professional development

Many authors believe CPD to be central to teacher professionalism and develop-ment as well as to the improvement of learning and teaching in the 14–19 sector. Thompson and Williams (2007: 2) plainly state that 'We were led to teacher profes-sional development was the fundamental lever for improving student learning by a growing body of research on the influences on student learning, which shows that teacher quality trumps virtually all other influences on students' (Thompson and Williams, 2007: 2). Villeneuve-Smith, West and Bhinder (2009) quite simply believe that 'CPD changes everything'.

There is also recognition that CPD is a professional responsibility of teachers in the sector and, indeed, is an essential component of their own lifelong learning (Coffield, 2008; IfL, 2009; Scales et al., 2011). In addition to the lifelong learning aspect, Coffield (2008) points out that CPD is also a 'right' for professionals: 'CPD is a responsibility for all professionals but it is also a right. If "personalised" learning is the new government aim for all students, then it should apply equally to staff, who have their own learning needs, gaps and aspirations' (Coffield, 2007: 726). Further, if we believe that teachers in the sector should be helping students to become 'independent enquirers', 'creative thinkers' and 'self-managers', as suggested in the Personal, Learning and Thinking Skills Framework (QCA, 2007), then it seems appropriate that teachers should themselves develop these skills and abilities as part of their CPD.

This personalised approach to CPD is contrary to many existing models of 'best practice', for example the 'Gold Dust' resources which now gather dust on many staffroom shelves. Such 'best practice' materials and the implication that they are suitable for all students across a range of settings have been criticised (Scales et al., 2011) in that they appear to have been produced in 'context-free' environments and, therefore, have limited reference to, and use in, specific contexts. This recognition of the limited use of 'best practice' materials and methods underpins James and Biesta's (2007) 'cultural approach' to learning. The authors suggest the development of a cultural approach to understanding learning and argue for the transformation of 'learning cultures' in further education. They conclude that all places of learning are particular and located in their own contexts and, whilst there will be similarities, are all unique. Rather than simply accepting imported 'best practice', '. . . the cultural approach helps us to see that the improvement of learning cultures always asks for contextualised judgement rather than for general recipes' (James and Biesta, 2007). Such general recipes and best practice solutions have often been delivered to teachers in attendance at large-scale staff development events in a 'sheep-dip' approach to CPD (Scales et al., 2011).

A move away from 'best practice' approaches and a cultural approach to learning and CPD implies a move to more localised and contextualised solutions to learning, alongside the development of individual teachers and groups of teachers researching and developing their own practice and, as appropriate, forming communities of practice in which they can experiment with new ideas and methods (Wenger, 1998). This 'teacher as researcher' approach has, possibly, been neglected in the prevailing atmosphere of audit, managerialism and best practice, but it does have some interesting antecedents. Wiseman (1948), writing about the teacher and research in the context of the birth of the National Foundation for Educational Research, recognises the importance of large-scale research 'planned and controlled by expert and experienced research workers' but, more importantly, suggests that such large-scale research:

does not mean that no other problems exist, problems which, while not urgent and pressing at the 'policy level', are nevertheless urgent and pressing at the classroom level. And in the gradual solution of such problems the individual research worker has an essential part to play.

(Wiseman, 1948: 116)

Further to this, Stenhouse (1975) writes of the 'extended professional' who is characterised by 'a capacity for autonomous professional development through systematic self-study' and 'testing of ideas by classroom research procedures' (Stenhouse, 1975: 144).

Wells (1986) suggests:

Every teacher needs to become his or her own theory builder, but a builder of theory that grows out of practice and has as its aim to improve the quality of practice. For too long, 'experts' from outside the classroom have told teachers what to think and what to do.

(Wells, 1986: 221)

Teachers teach; researchers research. For many teachers in the sector, this proposition remains axiomatic and the notion of themselves as researchers seems alien, something arcane and complex that academics do to produce conclusions and propositions which may, or may not, filter down to teachers. Teachers are frequently the subjects of research, less frequently the initiators of it. Stenhouse suggests, 'It is not enough that teachers' work should be studied; they need to study it themselves.' (Stenhouse, 1975: 143).

There is a significant amount of literature concerned with action research and practitioner researchers (Bell, 2005; Denscombe, 2007; Cohen, Manion and Morrison, 2007). This kind of practitioner research, carried out by teachers who encounter learning and teaching problems or a need for change, is particularly aimed at providing solutions at a local level which may also have wider application, and as McNiff and Whitehead state:

Action research is a form of enquiry that enables practitioners everywhere to investigate and evaluate their work. They ask, 'What am I doing? What do I need to improve? How do I improve it?' Their accounts of practice show how they are trying to improve their own learning and influence the learning of others.

(Mcniff and Whitehead, 2006: 7)

Within the 14–19 education sector it has been suggested by various sources, most notably Lynch et al. (2010) and Wolf (2011), that vocationally based knowledge is missing within the teaching workforce. 'Teachers derive their professional identity from (mostly combinations of) the ways they see themselves as subject matter experts, pedagogical experts, and didactical experts' (Beijaard, Verloop, and Vermunt, 2000: 751). It is further suggested that within Europe these three concepts are commonly used to indicate what teachers should do and know. If we examine these three areas in relation to the 14–19 teacher, we find that within subject matter knowledge, the ability to transform the knowledge into something that is teachable and that teachers should have a deep and full understanding of the subject area provides the professional bias (Calderhead, 1996).

So what should the 14–19 teacher do for their own CPD?

It is important to recognise that teachers within the 14–19 sector recognise the changing nature of their sector and that subject knowledge in vocational education can very quickly become outdated. In such a rapidly changing environment teachers need to become researchers and developers of their own practice within their own personal context. This includes dialogue with fellow professionals and opportunities to be part of wider communities of practice.

The following section provides some suggestions for starting CPD.

Reflective practice

Reflective practice is one of the fundamental elements for self-improvement and a good starting point for CPD. Moon defines reflective practice as 'a set of abilities and skills, to indicate the taking of a critical stance, an orientation to problem solving or state of mind' (1999: 63). The Higher Education Academy defines it as 'an approach that promotes autonomous learning that aims to develop students' understanding and critical thinking skills'.

Most models of the reflective process are presented as cyclical models and this section will explore some of these models and how they can be used as a form of CPD.

The simplest model is that of Greenaway (2002) which is based on a three-stage model of plan, do, review, based on the quality improvement cycle found in business. If we use this model in the classroom we are effectively using common-sense reflection as described by Moon (1999). What it fails to include is the learning element from the review, however, as a starting point it is a useful model as a basis to build upon.

Activity

Consider a recent classroom activity that you have completed with your learners.

Devise a set of common-sense reflection questions that you can use to identify learning points for you.

The second model that you can use is the four-stage model, which takes the Greenaway model one step further and includes the element of drawing conclusions. The most well-known model here is that of Kolb (1976). Essentially this model of reflection is based on experiential learning and relies on the learner (you) planning,

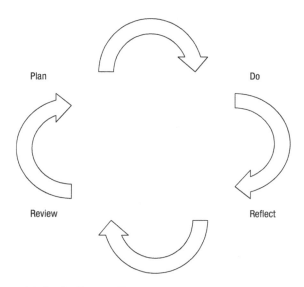

FIGURE 9.2 Kolb's model of reflective practice

doing, reviewing and drawing conclusions before repeating the cycle. This model not only questions the 'what' within an event but expands this by asking 'why' to evaluate and analyse the event.

The previous two models are examples for you to consider for your own CPD. I do not intend to go into any depth around reflective practice as there are many specialised texts that you could refer to. Suffice to say that as a teacher, reflection in action, on action and for action are areas that should be considered. In-action reflection takes place during an activity or session and results in adjusting times, plans etc accordingly. On-action reflection follows a lesson and considers what worked, what didn't, and what could be done differently. For-action reflection is the basis for future planning.

Action research as a concept investigates practice with a view to making improvements. It is usually a hands-on practical approach and can be undertaken either individually or in small communities of practice. Action research would normally involve providing solutions to real-life problems and is an active rather than passive process.

The following case study is an abstract from a larger piece of work undertaken by a local FE college as part of a CPD project with a university.

Consider how you would approach an issue currently facing you in your teaching.

Case study

The 'Yammer' project was conducted in an FE college delivering the Professional Graduate Certificate in Education and Certificate in Education to a number of in-service teacher trainees. Participants were asked to write weekly reflections for 13 weeks as part of their first module before being introduced to the social media platform, Yammer.

The project focused on whether social media augments reflection and thereby professionalism. The project aimed to:

1 Explore how social media, specifically the use of Yammer, impacts on the traditional notion/ structure of reflection.
2 Analyse the extent to which reflection develops aspects of professionalism in teacher trainees.
3 Review trainee experiences using different formats of reflection and make recommendations for future development of teacher education programmes of study.

The project identified that the benefits of using Yammer for trainees were:

1 Trainees were able to bottle learning and record incidents immediately (often within their working day) through the use of social media.
2 A greater understanding and empathy with each other through the sharing of reflections (they do not feel so alone on their teaching journey).
3 Sharing of good practices developed aspects of professionalism.
4 Variety: ability to make short and extended contributions.
5 Motivation and engagement: trainees were actively using the resource and for most it became part of their daily routine.

The final recommendations from the action research project suggested the following:

1 Making Yammer training part of the induction process for the Teacher Education programme; this will have a positive impact on the learner experience as it will allow those who are interested in technology to record their experience using an accessible format.
2 Yammer to be made accessible across the partnership and college, to link various groups and create networks between academic staff, mentors and trainees.
   Introducing mentor-to-learner networks to help trainees to benefit from professional experience and subject specific advice and guidance.
   Links to CPD as a means of developing professionalism and best practices within organisations.

Consider your organisation what action research projects there could be that would help you develop your own skills and knowledge?

Planning your own CPD

There are several different approaches to planning your own individual CPD, and you as the teacher will know what you require to develop either your subject knowledge or your role as the teacher.

One of the easiest models to use is a CPD cycle based upon experiential learning. This cycle has five distinct stages as highlighted below.

Step 1: Reflect upon your role, subject and specialism in the context within which you work. For the 14–19 age phase this could be around new legislation, new qualifications or new government priorities.

Step 2: Undertake an analysis of your key priorities. This may be based on performance reviews, student feedback, lesson observations, new curriculum.

Step 3: Create an individualised learning plan. This should identify activities, together with a timeline and information on how you will ensure and measure your progress.

Step 4: Undertake the activities identified.

Step 5: Reflect on the activities and evaluate.

Suggested CPD activities

The following section will consider some CPD activities that you may wish to engage with to support your own professional development.

Reading

Simply reading can be a very cost effective and efficient way of developing skills and knowledge. Consider what sources there are available to you from educational journals and newspapers (*TES*, *The Guardian*, etc) to texts on learning and teaching to support your pedagogic needs. In addition there will be numerous texts and sources to support you in developing your own subject area.

Team-teaching

Working with a more experienced teacher to team-teach can provide a wealth of CPD opportunities for new or less experienced teachers, and indeed new teachers can also provide more experienced teachers with new ideas for delivery. Team-teaching can support pedagogic approaches, dealing with disruptive behaviour, and subject enhancement to name but a few. Likewise, work-shadowing can also be a useful activity to look at how others deal with classes, students, subjects and situations.

Communities of practice/action learning sets

Groups of like-minded people coming together to discuss how to develop their own professional practice can be a very powerful tool. It can also lead to action research projects, such as the Yammer project discussed earlier.

Peer visits to other organisations

Again, this is relatively simple and cost effective, but can provide you with the opportunity to experience other institutions and their ways of working, which may then in turn inspire your own practice. It's also an excellent opportunity to share good practice with other like-minded professionals who may not work in exactly the same setting as you.

Examiner/assessor roles

Many awarding bodies seek staff to be involved in assessment processes during the summer months. This may be as simple as exam script marking or it may mean visits to other institutions to verify assessment decisions and moderate process. These opportunities are very worthwhile in that not only do they give insight to awarding body requirements but they enable you to benchmark yourself and your institution against other organisations offering similar programmes.

Employer links

With vocational education it is imperative that the teacher remains current in his or her subject knowledge. Therefore, maintaining strong links with employers is essential not only for industry updating but for skills updating. Many subject areas require teachers to return to industry once a year to update their own professional and personal skills.

Sector skills councils

Sector skills councils (SSC) are employer-led organisations that were set up to support employers in developing and managing apprenticeship standards, reduce skills gaps and to improve the skills of the workforce. As a teacher, linking with the sector skills councils will also support you with your own CPD. The following list was correct as of January 2015:

- *Building Futures Group* – facilities management, housing, property, cleaning and parking
- *Cogent* – nuclear, chemicals, polymers, petroleum, life sciences and pharmaceuticals
- *Construction Skills* – construction
- *Creative and Cultural Skills* – craft, cultural heritage, design, jewellery, literature, music, performing arts and visual arts
- *Creative Skillset* – tv, film, radio, interactive media, animation, computer games
- *Energy and Utility Skills* – gas, power, waste management and water industries
- *e-skills UK* – business and information technology
- *Financial Skills Partnership* – finance, accountancy and financial services
- *Improve* – food and drink manufacturing and associated supply chains
- *Institute of the Motor Industry* – retail motor industry
- *Lantra* – land management and production, animal health and welfare and environmental industries
- *People 1st* – hospitality, leisure, passenger transport, travel and tourism

- *Semta* – science, engineering and manufacturing technologies
- *Skills for Care and Development* – social care, children, early years and young people's workforces in the uk
- *Skills for Health* – uk health
- *Skills for Justice* – community justice, courts services, custodial care, fire and rescue, forensic science, policing and law enforcement and prosecution services
- *Skills for Logistics* – freight logistics and wholesaling industry
- *SkillsActive* – sport, fitness, outdoors, playwork, caravans and hair and beauty
- *SummitSkills* – building services, engineering

Subject associations

Subject associations are normally membership organisations, often registered charities, whose mission is to further the teaching and learning of a specific subject in schools, colleges and universities. They are independent of government and believe very strongly in supporting teachers in their subject specialism

For a list of current associations visit:

www.subjectassociation.org.uk/members_links.aspx (accessed November 2015).

Activity

Consider the CPD cycle and possible activities discussed above and start to create your own development plan. What other types of activity could you include?

Measuring the impact of your CPD

The overarching principle of CPD is to create a positive impact on teaching and learning, and as a result improve student retention and achievement and enhance your own professionalism and expertise. We should always reflect on the impact that any CPD activity has had on our practice, whether positive impact, or in the worse-case scenario, negative impact! Reflection is vital to the success of CPD and is in its own right a form of CPD. Consider the last CPD activity that you undertook. I would suggest that prior to embarking on the activity you should have considered what it was you wished to achieve and in what timescale. Following the activity, the natural closure of the loop would be to consider if you had achieved your initial objective and if not why not?

Activity

Review one of the CPD activities that you have undertaken during the last six months. What were your expected outcomes, for you as the teacher, for your students and how could you measure the impact?

Conclusion

The key characteristic of a professional is the ability for professional self-development through a process of reflection and self-audit. This chapter has explored some of the theories of CPD and examined how they can be applied to the role of a teacher. In this rapidly changing environment teachers need to become researchers and developers of their own practice. Therefore, it is imperative that as a teacher that you keep up to date with your own knowledge by maintaining, improving and broadening your own skills in your subject specialism.

References

Adams, K. & Hambright, G. (2005) 'Helping teachers become transformational leaders', *Academic Exchange Quarterly*, 9 (2): 90–94.

Beijaard, D., Verloop, N. & Vermunt, J. D. (2000) 'Teachers' perceptions of professional identity: an exploratory study from a personal knowledge perspective', *Teaching and Teacher Education*, 16: 749–764.

Bell, J. (2005) *Doing Your Research Project*. Buckingham: Open University Press.

Beyer, L.E. (2002) 'The politics of standardization: teacher education in the USA', *Journal of Education for Teaching*, 2 8(3): 239–245.

Boreham, N. (2002) 'Work process knowledge in technological and organizational development', in: Boreham, N., Samurçay, R. & Fischer, M. (eds) *Work Process Knowledge*. London: Routledge.

Boreham, N. (2004) 'A theory of collective competence: challenging the neoliberal individualisation of performance at work', *British Journal of Educational Studies*, 52 (1): 5–17.

Boreham, N., Samurçay, R. & Fischer, M. (eds.) (2002) *Work Process Knowledge*. London: Routledge.

Calderhead, J. (1996) 'Teachers: beliefs and knowledge', in Berliner D. C., & Calfee, R. C. (eds.) *Handbook of Educational Psychology*. New York: Macmillan Library Reference.

Coffield, F., Edward, S., Finlay, L., Hodgson, A., Spours, K. & Steer, R. (2008) *Improving Learning and Inclusion: The Impact of Policy and Policy-making on Post-compulsory Education*. London: Routledge.

Cohen, L., Manion, L. & Morrison, K. (2007) *Research Methods in Education* (6th Ed). London: Routledge Falmer.

Denscombe, M. (2007) *The Good Research Guide*. Maidenhead: McGraw-Hill.

Eaton, P. T. & Carbonne, R. E. (2008) 'Asking those who know: A collaborative approach to continuing professional development', *Teacher Development,* 12(3): 261–270.

Evans, L. (2002) 'What is teacher development?', *Oxford Review of Education,* 28 (1): 123–137.

Grangeat, M. (2004) 'Effets de l'organisation de la situation de travail sur les compétences curriculaires des enseignants', *Revue Française de Pédagogie.* 147: 27–42.

Grangeat, M. & Gray, P. (2007) 'Factors influencing teachers' professional competence development', *Journal of Vocational Education and Training,* 59 (4): 485–501.

Greenaway, R. (2002) *Experiential Learning Cycles.* www.reviewing.co.uk/research/learning.cycles.htm

Hargreaves, D. (1998) *Creative Professionalism: The Role of Teachers in the Knowledge Society.* London: Demos.

Hegarty, S. (2000) 'Teaching as a knowledge-based activity', *Oxford Review of Education,* 26: 451–455.

Hoban, G. F. (2002) *Teacher Learning for Educational Change.* Buckingham: Open University Press.

IfL (2009) *IfL Review of CPD: Making a Difference for Teachers, Trainers and Learners.* London: The Institute for Learning.

James, D. & Biesta, G. (2007) *Improving Learning Cultures in Further Education.* Abingdon: Routledge.

Kennedy, A. (2005) 'Models of continuing professional development: a framework for analysis', *Journal of In-service Education,* 31(2): 235–250.

Kolb, D. A. (1976). *Experiential Learning: Experience as the Source of Learning and Development.* New Jersey: Prentice Hall.

Lynch, S., McCrone, T., Wade, P., Featherstone, G., Evans, K., Golden, S. & Haynes, G. (2010). *National Evaluation of Diplomas: The First Year of Delivery* (DCSF Research Brief 220). London: DCSF.

McNally, J., Boreham, N. & Cope, P. (2004) 'Showdown at the last chance saloon: research meets policy in early professional learning'. Paper presented at the annual ECER Conference, Crete.

McNiff, J. & Whitehead, J. (2006) *Action Research in Organisations.* London: Routledge.

Moon, J. (1999) *Learning Journals: A Handbook for Academics, Students and Professional Development.* London: Kogan Page.

Pastré, P. (2004) 'Le rôle des concepts pragmatiques dans la gestion de situations problèmes: le casdes régleurs en plasturgie', in Samurçay R. & Pastré, P. (eds) *Recherches en Didactique Professionnelle.* Toulouse: Octarès.

Patrick, F., Forde, C. & McPhee, A. (2003) 'Challenging the "new professionalism": from managerialism to pedagogy', *Journal of In-Service Education.* 29 (2):237–253.

Peel, D. (2005) 'Dual professionalism: facing the challenges of continuing professional development in the workplace', *Reflective Practice,* 6 (1): 123–140.

Qualifications and Curriculum Authority (QCA) (2007) *A Framework of Personal Learning and Thinking Skills.* London: QCA.

Rhodes, C. P. & Beneicke, S. (2003) 'Professional development support for poorly performing teachers: Challenges and opportunities for school managers in addressing teacher learning needs', *Journal of In-Service Education*, 29 (1): 121–138.

Robert, A. & Rogalski, J. (2005) 'A cross-analysis of the mathematics teacher's activity: an example in a French 10th-grade class', *Educational Studies in Mathematics*, 59: 269–298.

Samurçay, R. & Vidal-Gomel, C. (2002) 'The contribution of work process knowledge to competence in electrical maintenance', In Boreham, N., Samurçay, R. & Fischer M. (eds) *Work Process Knowledge*. London: Routledge.

Scales, P., Pickering, J., Senior. L., Headley. K., Garner, P. & Boulton, H. (2011) *Continuing Professional Development in the Lifelong Learning Sector*. Buckingham: Open University Press.

Smyth, J. (1991) *Teachers as Collaborative Learners*. Buckingham: Open University Press.

Stenhouse, L. (1975) *An Introduction to Curriculum Research and Development*. London: Heinemann.

Thompson, M. & Williams, D. (2007) *Tight but Loose: Scaling up Teacher Professional Development in Diverse Contexts*. Princeton, NJ: Educational Testing Service.

Villegas-Reimers, E. & Reimers, F. (2000) 'The Professional Development of Teachers as Lifelong Learners: models. practices and factors that influence it'. Paper prepared for *The Board on International Comparative Studies in Education BISCE of the National Research Council*, Washington.

Villeneuve-Smith, F., West, C. & Bhinder, B. (2009) *Rethinking Continuing Professional Development in Further Education – Eight Things You Already Know About CPD*. London: Learning and Skills Network.

Wenger, E. (1998) *Communities of Practice: Learning, Meaning and Identity*. Cambridge: Cambridge University Press.

Wells, G. (1986) *The Meaning Makers*. London: Hodder and Stoughton.

Wiseman, S. (1948) 'The marking of English grammar composition', *British Journal of Educational Psychology*, 19(3): 200–209.

Wolf, A. (2011) *A Review of Vocational Education – The Wolf Report*. London: DfE.

Further reading

Cohen, L. & Manion, L. (1992) *Research Methods in Education* (3rd ed). London: Routledge.

Day, C. (1994) 'Planning for the professional development of teachers and schools: A principled approach', in Simpson, T.A. (ed) *Teacher Educators' Handbook*. Queensland: Queensland University of Technology.

IoE (2010) Institute of Education Archives. www.ioe.ac.uk/is (Accessed 26 May 2015).

Kennedy, A. (2007) 'Continuing professional development (CPD) policy and the discourse of teacher professionalism in Scotland', *Research Papers in Education*, 22 (1): 95–111.

Moon, J. (2004) *A Handbook of Reflective and Experiential Learning: Theory and Practice*. London: Routledge.

Ofsted (2004) *Developing New Vocational Pathways: Final Report on the Introduction of new GCSEs*. London: Ofsted.

Ofsted (2005) *Work-related Learning: The Story so Far*. London: Ofsted.

Robinson, W. (2014) *A Learning Profession? Teachers and Their Professional Development in England and Wales 1920–2000*. Netherlands: Sense.

Robson, J. (1998) 'A Profession in Crisis: status, culture and identity in the further education college', *Journal of Vocational Education and Training*, 50 (4): 585–607.

Sachs, J. (2001) 'Rethinking the practice of teacher professionalism', in Day, C., Fernadez, A., Hague, T. & Moller, J. (eds.) *The Life and Work of Teachers*. London: Falmer Press.

10

Legislation working

Introduction

There are many pieces of legislation that affect education in the United Kingdom, and no doubt since the publication of this text there have been several more papers been presented to government, both education-specific (at the time of writing the Education Green Paper had just been released) and relating to other elements of health and safety law that impact upon everyday practice in the classroom. This text is not intended to provide a full and thorough discussion of education acts and legislation, as there are many texts available should you feel that would be of use to you. Rather, this chapter will consider some of the key pieces of legislation that have impacted upon the 14–19 sector both from an organisational perspective and a teaching perspective. The first section will discuss some of the main acts that are impacting on 14–19 organisational structures and the second section will concentrate on the laws that affect working practices.

Educational acts affecting 14–19 provision 2006–2015

Education and Skills Act (2008)

In 2008, the then Coalition Government passed the Education and Skills Act. The main thrust of this act and its impact upon 14–19 education was the requirement for all young people in England to remain in education or training, at least part-time, until they are 17 years old by 2013, and that by 2015, all young people will have to stay on in education or training, at least part-time, until they are 18 years old.

For the 14–19 sector this means that young people have to be in one of the following:

- full-time education or training, including school, college and home education;
- work-based learning, such as an apprenticeship, or
- part-time education or training or volunteering more than 20 hours a week.

This act has had major implications for the sector and has, in my opinion, created a stronger need for a better balance between traditional academic qualifications and the more skills-based qualifications. According to a recent newspaper article, whilst the government are keen to develop apprenticeships the number of young people between the ages of 16–18 being taken on as an apprentice still remain low, with very few being encouraged into vocational routes (the *Guardian*, October 2015). For the 14–19 sector this creates opportunities to develop strong links with employers to encourage more people to take up apprenticeships.

Education Act (2011)

The Education Act (2011) is quite a lengthy document, much of which deals with governance and the rights of students and teachers.

The key areas that I would like to bring your attention to are that the act required schools to secure independent and impartial careers advice for pupils from the age of 14 (See Chapter 12 on IAG and employability) and ended the national entitlement to access the Diploma qualification (now extinct!) for 16–18 year olds in Key Stage 4.

The other main areas that affect 14–19 provision are the sections surrounding FE and academies.

Academies

The act sets out two key academies, 16–19 and mainstream. Within the 16–19 section education is taken to mean, vocational, social, physical and recreational training, either full time or part time. The act removed the need for an academy to have a named specialism, although you may still hear of 'dance academies', 'engineering academies', etc. The key point to be aware of here is that under current legislation you are not required, although it is deemed good practice, to have a teaching qualification to teach in an academy.

FE colleges

The key change for FE colleges was the inclusion of apprenticeships in the FE sector. (For further information on apprenticeships, see Chapter 3.)

Education Act 2014

The Education Act (2014) is quite a lengthy document, much of which surrounds governance and the rights of students and teachers.

The key areas that I would like to bring your attention to are that the act required schools to secure independent and impartial careers advice for pupils from the age of 14 (see Chapter 12 on IAG and employability) and ended the national entitlement to access the Diploma qualification (now extinct!) for 16–18 year olds at Key Stage 4.

The other main areas that affect 14–19 provision are the sections surrounding FE and academies.

Children and Families Act 2014

The Children and Families Act (2014) has been introduced to deliver better support for families – legislating to break down barriers, bureaucracy and delays which stop vulnerable children getting the help they need. The act introduced a new assessment process for children with special educational needs and disability (SEND) up to the age of 25. This process replaced statements and learning difficulty assessments with a new health care plan (HCP). The key element of this change is that children aged 16–25 are now covered by the legislation. As a teacher of 14–19 you may come across students with a HCP and need to be aware that this document entitles the student and/or the parents to individual support, a budget and regular meetings with the educational establishment. The basic goals of the act are to give families a greater involvement in decisions about their children, and to support and to encourage social care, education and health services to work together more closely in supporting those with special needs or disabilities.

As part of the changes, local authorities are required to publish a 'local offer' setting out what support is available to families with children who have disabilities or SEN. The local offer should also explain how families can request personal budgets, make complaints and access more specialist help. For anyone working in the 14–19 sector you need to ensure that there is a SEN contact who will work with any of your learners that fall into this category.

Activity

Go to the following web link, which gives further information on the legislation, and consider what it might mean to you if you teach in a school 14–16 or post-16.

www.educationbusinessuk.net/features/important-questions-send-reforms

---

Legislation and working practices for the 14–19 teacher, tutor and trainer

Discrimination in education

There are two laws that seek to promote equality of opportunity for the disabled learner by banning disability discrimination and giving enforceable legal rights to them. These are the Disability Discrimination Act 1995, updated in 2010 to the Equality Act, and the Special Educational Needs & Disability Code of Practice that came out of the Children and Families Act (2014).

Under the Disability Discrimination Act (DDA) it is against the law for a school or other education provider to treat disabled students unfavorably. This includes:

- 'direct discrimination', e.g. refusing admission to a student because of disability;
- 'indirect discrimination', e.g. only providing application forms in one format that may not be accessible;
- 'discrimination arising from a disability', e.g. a disabled student is prevented from going outside at break time because it takes too long to get there;
- 'harassment', e.g. a teacher shouts at a disabled student for not paying attention when the student's disability stops them from easily concentrating;
- victimisation, e.g. suspending a disabled student because they've complained about harassment.

It is the responsibility of the educational establishment to ensure that it makes reasonable adjustments to accommodate its disabled students. There are some exceptions in order to allow for the maintenance of faith schools and single-sex schools; some disabled pupils and pupils with a statement of 'special educational needs' may be segregated in special schools, and schools may temporarily or permanently exclude pupils for disciplinary reasons.

However, the reasonable adjustments may mean as a teacher you need to consider any additional support a student may need, such as writers, signers or even something as simple as a large font on any handouts. You may also need to consider whether the assessments you are planning for a particular subject are appropriate or whether you need to have a different assessment to enable a disabled student to participate without any disadvantage.

Activity

Consider the assessments you provide for any of your modules, are they easily accessible to hearing-impaired, visually-impaired or speech-impaired students? What could you do differently?

Are there any other types of disability that may be disadvantaged with your proposed assessments?

Safeguarding

Safeguarding legislation exists to protect children from maltreatment, prevent impairment of children's health or development, ensure that children are growing up in circumstances consistent with the provision of safe and effective care, take action to enable all children and young people to have the best outcomes. Any child can be hurt, put at risk of harm or abused, regardless of their age, gender, religion or ethnicity.

the action we take to promote the welfare of children and protect them from harm is everyone's responsibility. Everyone who comes into contact with children and families has a role to play.

(HM Government 2013)

In England the law states that people who work with children have to keep them safe. This safeguarding legislation is set out in The Children Act (1989) and (2004). It also features in the United Nations Convention on the Rights of the Child (to which the UK is a signatory) and sets out the rights of children to be free from abuse. The Government also provides guidance in their document *Working Together to Safeguard Children*, (2013).

Jobs that involve caring for, supervising or being in sole charge of children or adults require an enhanced disclosure and barring service check (previously called an enhanced criminal records bureau check). This includes anyone teaching in schools or colleges, or teaching vulnerable adults.

The following list provides some of the facts surrounding the safeguarding legisation.

- Almost one in five children today has experienced serious physical abuse, sexual abuse or severe physical or emotional neglect at some point in their lifetime.
- One in ten children in the UK has been neglected.
- There were a total of 21,493 sexual offences against children recorded by police in the UK in 2011/2012.
- One in 14 children in the UK has been physically abused.
- Around one in five children in the UK has been exposed to domestic violence.
- On average, every week in the UK, at least one child is killed at the hands of another person.
- Over a third of serious case reviews involves a child under one.
- For every child placed on a child protection plan or the child protection register, it is estimated that there are another eight children who are suffering from abuse and neglect and not getting the support they need.
- There were 68,840 looked after children in England on 31 March 2014.
- Deaf and disabled children are more than three times more likely to be abused or neglected than non-disabled children.

(www.safenetwork.org.uk/, accessed October 2015)

As a teacher working in the 14–19 sector you need to be aware of safeguarding as a potential issue and should be aware of some of the signs that your learners may be at risk. In today's society many 14–19 year old boys and girls either are or have been the victims of internet abuse, whether it be cyberbullying, 'trolling' or sexual grooming.

The key pieces of national and local safeguarding children guidance are:

- Keeping Children Safe in Education, DFE 2015;
- Working Together to Safeguard Children, DFE 2015;
- What To Do if You're Worried a Child is Being Abused, DFE 2015;
- Information Sharing: Advice for Practitioners Providing Safeguarding Services, DFE 2015;
- SSCB (Safeguarding Children's Board) Child Protection & Safeguarding Procedures Manual;
- Early Years Foundation Stage, DFE 2014;
- Disqualification under the Childcare Act (2006).

Activity

For your organisation there are several implications and guidelines that you need to follow. Your educational establishment should:

- ensure that you follow all safeguarding responsibilities, both as an individual and according to your organisation's specific policies;
- identify staff to take on specific roles within the context of safeguarding, such as safeguarding lead, designated teacher, a governor (if appropriate to take on the safeguarding remit);
- provide training for all staff, including temporary, supply or agency staff;
- audit and monitor any child who has a safeguarding need;
- provide curriculum-based awareness education of, for example, e-safety, healthy relationships, abuse, neglect, bullying, etc.;
- provide parents and guardians access to policies, through the web and within any prospectus;
- keep safeguarding records confidential and securely stored, share information appropriately with other agencies, and attend meetings and conferences as required;
- provide training to ensure that all staff are confident and know what to do should any allegations be made against staff or other adults.

Contact your safeguarding office and look at the safeguarding policy. What are your individual responsibilities as a teacher? What CPD might you need?

There are several other laws and acts that are very closely linked to the safeguarding agenda that you need to be cognizant of working in education.

The Prevent agenda

From July 2015 all schools, colleges and universities, plus early years providers have a statutory duty under section 26 of the Counter-Terrorism and Security Act 2015, to have 'due regard to the need to prevent people from being drawn into terrorism'. The Prevent duty is consistent with schools' and childcare providers' existing responsibilities, and as a teacher you will be expected to be aware and indeed compliant with the requirements. Ofsted's revised common inspection framework for education, skills and early years, which comes into effect from 1 September 2015, makes specific reference to the need to have safeguarding arrangements to promote pupils' welfare and prevent radicalisation and extremism. Radicalisation refers to the process by which a person comes to support terrorism and extremism. These ideas can include violent far right views, animal rights activism, and religious fundamentalism.

The Prevent duty for the teacher

Under the Prevent legislation you have a duty to be vigilant and observant in your exchanges with student. Factors that could make a student vulnerable include:

- pressure from peers, other people or the internet;
- crime against them or their involvement in crime;
- anti-social behaviour and bullying;
- family tensions;
- race or hate crime;
- lack of self-esteem or identity;
- personal or political grievances.

As a teacher you need to be aware of potential tensions and support your learners through engaging them in debate and discussion, wherever possible linked to the curriculum and subject area, and to ensure that your learners are safeguarded against material when accessing the internet for their studies.

Activity

Go to the following articles to get further information about the Prevent agenda. What is your organisation implementing to comply with the agenda?

www.bbc.co.uk/news/uk-28939555
www.preventforschools.org/?category_id=40
www.safecampuscommunities.ac.uk/the-prevent-agenda
www.theguardian.com/uk-news/2015/mar/09/anti-radicalisation-prevent-strategy-a-toxic-brand

---

Female genital mutilation

This is another area that could impact upon you as a teacher under the wider umbrella of safeguarding.

Female genital mutilation (FGM) comprises all procedures involving partial or total removal of the external female genitalia or other injury to the female genital organs.

FGM is illegal in the UK and mandatory reporting to the Police commenced in October 2015. It is classified as a form of child abuse for girls under 18 years old, with long-lasting harmful consequences. For an educator it is important to know that girls who are threatened with, or who have undergone FGM may withdraw from education, restricting their educational and personal development. They may feel unable to go against the wishes of their parents and consequently may suffer emotionally as well as physically.

Signs to look out for in the classroom

As a teacher you will know your students some of the signs to look out for which may indicate safeguarding issues, including FGM, include:

- learners appear anxious, depressed and withdrawn;
- educational performance, aspirations or motivation may decline;
- absenteeism.

As a teacher it is worth knowing that most at-risk incidents occur during the summer holiday, so you may wish to look out for any personality changes in the summer term, and when girls return to school or college in the autumn.

Work-related learning for 14–19 vocational students

Work-related learning and the law has been in existence since 2004. The 2010 publication *Work-related Learning Guide* (DCSF, 2010) points out:

> *Work-related learning (WRL) has an outstanding track record on health and safety and everyone wants to keep it that way. Changes to the curriculum and the new Diplomas means more work-related learning, greater employment involvement, more contact with different people and more movement of young people between different locations. Keeping young people safe in this environment will require continued careful attention and good management.*
>
> *(DCSF, 2010: 22)*

This clearly demonstrates that the educational organisation, school or college has the primary 'duty of care' for their learners at **all** times – including times when learners are involved in work experience or other off-site work-related learning. Moreover, the home learning base/school has the responsibility to ensure that:

- placements are vetted by a competent person; and
- their learners are prepared and briefed generally about health and safety and understand how to identify hazards, and the sort of control measures that can be put in place to reduce the risk of injury or accident.

An example of activities that could be classed as WRL can be found in Appendix 1.

FE Colleges, employers and work-based learning providers have responsibility for the health, safety and welfare of everyone on their premises, including any learners who are there or engaged in activities there which may be organised. These responsibilities include:

- complying with child protection legislation;
- checking their insurers are aware of the implications of their involvement with work-related learning and, in particular, 14–16 year old learners;
- agreeing and implementing workable attendance, reporting, monitoring and emergency procedures in partnership with the home learning base/school;
- supporting their staff in adjusting to teaching young people by organising training and establishing workable and effective policies; and
- complying with legislation and good practice on data protection.

All home learning bases/schools/FE colleges have a 'duty of care' for their learners. Legislation, guidance and judgements resulting from inquests, enquiries, criminal prosecutions, as well as civil actions consistently focus on the home learning base's/school's/FE college's position as the body with the primary duty of care for their charges (i.e. learners). Consequently, when there is a decision to offer any off-site, curricular or extra-curricular activity, it is imperative that senior management and staff responsible for operational processes and practices related to work-related learning formally consider whether there is any increased risk to the health, safety and welfare of their learners, staff or others who may be involved.

Health and safety/risk assessments in education

Under DfE legislation all schools and colleges need a health and safety policy. The elements that should be included on the policy depend upon the size of the school or college and the nature of any risk associated with their activities.

The HSE website includes the following which should be included in any health and safety policy:

- a general statement of policy;
- who is responsible to do what (delegation of tasks); and
- arrangements to establish, monitor and review measures needed to meet satisfactory health and safety standards.

In addition, the HSE lists a range of activities that a school or a college could include. The following list is a snapshot that may be appropriate within 14–19 education:

- consultation arrangements with employees (work placements);
- policy and procedures for off-site visits, including residential visits and any school-led adventure activities;
- dealing with health and safety emergencies – procedures and contacts;
- first aid and supporting medical needs;
- workplace safety for teachers, pupils and visitors (in particular for some vocational subjects, e.g. engineering).

In addition, the nature of 14–19 and vocational education may mean that you are taking your learners on visits.

As a teacher involved in visits you need to be aware of your position of trust and professionality when considering venues. Risk assessments will need to be completed and should include the following:

- transport issues;
- first aid and medication arrangements for staff and students;
- any specific safeguarding issues relating to a student included on the visit;
- if site security and surveillance is appropriate;
- staff-to-child ratios, gender issues, and disability access and support;
- intimate care and personal hygiene issues;
- fire practice, health and safety issues;
- consideration of any other needs of the students that you are aware of;
- the suitability of bedrooms for overnight stays, taking into account separate rooms for boys and girls, and the location of staff bedrooms to ensure adequate supervision.

Disclosure and Barring Service (DBS) of convictions and cautions

The Disclosure and Barring Service (DBS) helps employers make safer recruitment decisions and prevent unsuitable people from working with vulnerable groups, including children. It replaces the Criminal Records Bureau (CRB) and Independent Safeguarding Authority (ISA). The DBS legislation came into effect on 29 May 2013.

The DBS' statutory responsibilities are:

- to process requests for criminal records checks as defined by Part V of the Police Act 1997, for applications made in England and Wales;

- to decide whether it is appropriate for a person to be placed on or removed from a barred list under the Safeguarding Vulnerable Groups Act 2006 or Safeguarding Vulnerable Groups Order (Northern Ireland) 2007;
- to maintain the DBS children's barred list and the DBS adults' barred list for England, Wales and Northern Ireland.

All cautions and convictions for serious violent and sexual offences as well as a list of other specific offences are subject to disclosure where the safeguarding of children and vulnerable adults is involved. All convictions where a custodial sentence was given also remain subject to disclosure. As a teacher in either a school, academy or FE college that works with children 14–19 you will be expected to undergo a DBS check. Any disclosures that fall into the categories identified as inappropriate for working with children will mean that your teaching post is at risk. The full list of offences can be found on the DBS website. www.gov.uk/government/publications/dbs-list-of-offences-that-will-never-be-filtered-from-a-criminal-record-check (accessed 15 September 2015).

Teaching qualifications

The teaching qualification you require will vary depending upon the sector you are working in, and even then the boundaries are blurred with 14–19 education.

Traditionally, someone working in a school would require QTS (qualified teacher status), with or without a PGCE, overseen by the National College of Teaching. The traditional route would see the teacher having a first degree, followed by the teaching qualification. The FE sector has always been different to the school sector, despite several attempts to bring them closer together. A teacher in FE does not require a first degree, although it has become more common for this to be a requirement. They do not officially require a teaching qualification, but the majority of teachers do undertake this for their own professional development and to create a professional identity. Within this sector many teachers undertake either a Certificate in Education or PGCE Post-14, leading to QTLS (qualified teacher learning skills) through a process called professional formation. Under British law QTS and QTLS are deemed to be equivalent and teachers should be able to move between the compulsory schools sector and the traditional post-16 sector. Academies do not by current law require their staff to hold teaching qualifications.

Activity

If you don't already hold a teaching qualification, explore the options open to you within your sector.

You may wish to look at university-based qualifications, such as PGCE, Bachelor of Education (B. Ed.) or qualifications you can gain whilst in work, assessment only QTS programmes or PGCE type programmes, such as those delivered in SCITTS or a combination of the two, and look at school direct training as a further option.

Conclusion

Whilst not exhaustive this chapter has provided you with some of the key areas surrounding legislative responsibilities and the acts that have shaped the 14–19 sector as we know it today.

You may wish to look at the policies that your organisation has in place to identify other key areas of legislation that are likely to impact upon your practice.

References

DCSF (2010) *Work-related Learning Guide* (1st edition). Nottingham: DCSF.

HM Government (2013) *Working Together to Safeguard Children*. London: HM Government.

The Guardian (2015) 'Apprenticeships are no good unless done well' (26 October).

Further reading

The link below will take you to the latest policies that an educational establishment needs to have in place. Go to the link and compare it with what you know is in existence at your school or college.

www.gov.uk/government/publications/statutory-policies-for-schools

Collaborative practices in education

Introduction

Collaboration as a concept is nothing new within education. Schools and colleges have collaborated for many years across 14–19 provision. Likewise, colleges have collaborated with universities to provide programmes at levels 4 and 5. Within 14–19 and vocational education collaboration is essential to ensure that the learner has access to the work-based elements of the programme, whether that be work-placement, work-related learning opportunities or simply the apprenticeship place. In addition, schools and colleges are increasingly collaborating with similar institutions in a wide range of different types of collaborative activity, both formal and informal. The previous (coalition) government's commitment to inter-school collaboration was made clear in the Education White Paper *The Importance of Teaching* (DfE, 2010):

> *Schools working together leads to better results . . . Along with our best schools, we will encourage strong and experienced sponsors to play a leadership role in driving the improvement of the whole school system, including through leading more formal federations and chains.*

> *(DfE, 2010: 60)*

This chapter will explore some of the ways in which collaboration in the sector, either inter school, cross-phase or inter-college, can benefit learning and achievement for our young people.

Definitions of collaboration

There are many different definitions of collaboration, however the following two provide a good overview for educational purposes.

> *Collaboration must be focused on the needs of a local learning area rather than simply on the individual needs of one of the partners.*
>
> *(Hodgson, Spours and Wright, 2005)*

> *the act of two or more people or organizations working together for a particular purpose.*
>
> *(Oxford English Dictionary, 1989)*

It is evident from these two definitions that collaboration is a mutually beneficial arrangement between two or more stakeholders.

For schools in particular the term 'collaboration', when used to refer to inter-school working, can mean many different things. Other words you may hear to describe what is basically a collaborative agreement are: 'partnership', 'network', 'cluster', 'family', 'federation', 'engagement', to name but a few. You may also hear school collaborations within the guise of multi-academy trusts (MATS) as part of the move to create academies.

What is collaboration and what does it mean for 14–19 education?

As we have seen from the definitions, the word collaboration is used when there is an expected beneficial outcome by the collaborators. The more significant for each party the higher the commitment level and participation will be amongst the collaborators. Within education, and 14–19 education, collaboration is essential to ensure that young people are receiving a high-quality product. Unfortunately, in recent times the need for institutions to retain students, and therefore funding, may have meant collaboration has not been as effective as it could be. However, I would argue that this as a challenge could create a further problem in that students will just go elsewhere!

Successful collaboration has been described as synergy, where the sum is greater than all the parts (i.e. 2+2=5). This can be true if all collaborators are outcome driven, and have left their selfish interests behind. There are four key principles of collaboration: participation, transparency, communication and buy-in. One cannot function without the other – they are interdependent.

Case study

College Y collaborates with University X on a level 5 apprenticeship programme that is combined with a foundation degree. The college needs the partnership with the university as they do not have the full skill-base to deliver programmes at level 5. For the university the partnership provides some income and a pipeline of potential students who wish to complete their education and gain an honours degree following the level 5 programme. Within the partnership the university provides a framework of study and support for delivery to the college, all communicated through the virtual learning space.

Within the first two weeks of the course several students complain that they don't feel that they are being given the correct information and several of them decide to drop out and study elsewhere.

1   What do you think went wrong with the collaboration?
2   What could have been done differently to provide a better outcome?

In considering the case study and what went wrong you may wish to think about some of the following, which are key elements in successful collaborative relationships.

- **A shared purpose**: each organisaton should have shared goals and a shared understanding of the purpose of the relationship. Did the university understand the reasons that the college wished to collaborate – to provide an additional skills base?

- **Shared power**: each organisation should have something that they can bring to the partnership. In the above case the college had the students and the university the additional skill set. Did they realise that? Was there a sharing of power?

- **Shared view of interdependence**: this entails both parties understanding that both parties have to work together to meet the common goals.

- **Mutual respect and trust**: these two features need to be held not only in the beginning of collaboration but throughout the process. Part of this is making sure each organisation did what they said they would do. The university provided a framework and content but did they actually add to the skill set?

- **Shared control**: the previous steps help build up to shared control. This means making sure resources are shared in an efficient manner to accomplish the goal of the relationship. Were resources shared effectively?

- **Shared indicators of progress**: Having a conversation with the organisations about whether or not the purpose is being achieved is crucial. Checking up on progress and finding out what works and doesn't work will help better realise the overall goal. This means communication –not just via technology.

A brief historical overview of collaboration in the 14–19 arena

The concept of collaboration for 14–19 education was first introduced following the publication of 'The Education and Skills Implementation Plan' (DfES 2005). This document was concerned with the then 'National Entitlement Curriculum', which the Labour government at the time believed could only be offered through collaborative delivery with no single school being able to provide the full entitlement.

Advantages and challenges surrounding collaborative working

Collaboration may help secure many of the benefits of, and overcome many of the obstacles to the transformation of learning and teaching. Benefits can be gained from the interactions and sharing between students and between staff, and in developing teaching resources, creating learning-resources databases, and delivering courses.

The following highlights some of the advantages of working collaboratively.

- Mixed cohorts of learners – if you are working in collaboration cross-phase there are opportunities to have mixed cohorts from school-based and college-based provision in the same programme. This mix provides you with the opportunity to use the knowledge and experiences of each cohort to promote collaborative learning opportunities.

- Progression opportunities – collaborating cross-phase can result in better progression opportunities for your learners. For example, a college collaboration with a university may provide you with the opportunity for higher awards or some form of compact agreement that allows your learners to progress with slightly different conditions to others (i.e. slightly lower entry requirements).

- Improved access to resources – collaboration can provide a much wider and improved access to resources as both content and subject materials are shared, and learners have access to facilities at both organisations.

- Wider range of qualifications can be offered – collaboration can increase the curriculum offer enabling learners to study at different sites.

- Wider skill set – collaboration between two or more organisations can increase the knowledge and skills set for a particular subject and discipline area and staff can be encouraged teach across sites.

(Adapted from Senior 2010)

Activity

Which of the advantages listed above can you see taking place in any collaborations that you are currently involved with? Are there any others that you can add to this list?

However, whilst there are many advantages to working collaboratively there are also risks and challenges that you need to be aware of. There could be potential conflicts of interest if not all stakeholders have the same goals, damage to reputation, personality conflicts, lack of flexibility in timetables,to name but a few.

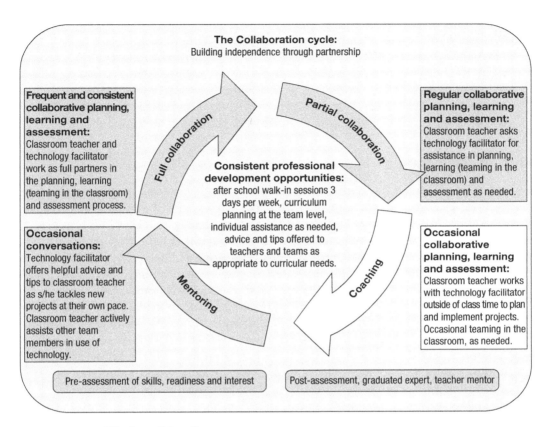

The Collaboration cycle:
Building independence through partnership

Frequent and consistent collaborative planning, learning and assessment: Classroom teacher and technology facilitator work as full partners in the planning, learning (teaming in the classroom) and assessment process.

Full collaboration

Partial collaboration

Regular collaborative planning, learning and assessment: Classroom teacher asks technology facilitator for assistance in planning, learning (teaming in the classroom) and assessment as needed.

Consistent professional development opportunities: after school walk-in sessions 3 days per week, curriculum planning at the team level, individual assistance as needed, advice and tips offered to teachers and teams as appropriate to curricular needs.

Occasional conversations: Technology facilitator offers helpful advice and tips to classroom teacher as s/he tackles new projects at their own pace. Classroom teacher actively assists other team members in use of technology.

Mentoring

Coaching

Occasional collaborative planning, learning and assessment: Classroom teacher works with technology facilitator outside of class time to plan and implement projects. Occasional teaming in the classroom, as needed.

Pre-assessment of skills, readiness and interest

Post-assessment, graduated expert, teacher mentor

FIGURE 11.1 Effective collaboration

Other forms of collaboration within 14–19 education

Teacher collaboration

While the traditional picture of the school teacher may feature a lone educator working in one classroom, a more collaborative approach can increase the likelihood that the students will succeed. Whether teachers are team-teaching – with two or more educators actually co-teaching one group or class of students – or they meet for team brainstorming and reflection sessions before or after school, creating a collaborative educational community can also help teacher effectiveness. Teaching in a collaborative environment allows educators to divide up the tasks at hand, making classroom activities more manageable. Teaching collaboratively provides a means for the exchanging of ideas. For example, teachers can share lesson-planning ideas or specific classroom activities during weekly meetings or discuss the positive and negative parts of a project for the other educators to learn from.

Parents

Just because parents aren't trained educators – at least, most of them aren't – doesn't mean they can't play a crucial role in the school or college setting. Creating meaningful partnerships with parents, and involving them in school activities as well as the students' studies, can help to improve educational outcomes such as grades and test scores, as well as building self-esteem and decreasing the dropout rate.

Student collaboration

Aside from teachers, administrators and parents collaborating to enhance the educational process, student teamwork scenarios can also have academic advantages. Group projects encourage learners to co-operate, improve social and interpersonal skills and help them to better understand the material at hand through discussion and a team learning effort. Learners must communicate effectively, work as a team and demonstrate self-discipline while working collaboratively with their peers. This, in turn, can increase their learning and maximise the educational experience. Student collaboration is also a form of teaching strategy available to you, that of collaborative learning. In simple terms collaborative learning is where two or more people learn or attempt to learn something together. As with other types of collaboration, collaborative learning makes use of an individual's knowledge, skills and resources. Collaborative learning involves students working together towards a common goal or purpose.

Collaborative learning activities can include collaborative writing, group projects, joint problem solving, debates, study teams, and other activities.

Reflecting on practice

In this chapter we have discussed the advantages and disadvantages of collaborative working and some of its key. Take a few minutes to reflect on the following questions for your own subject area and organisation:

- What are the qualities of successful collaborative practitioners?
- How might the characteristics of collaborative practitioners best be developed?
- What do collaborative practitioners do that ensure successful collaborative practice?
- Does collaborative practice require particular forms of leadership and if so what are they?

Conclusion

This chapter has explored some of the challenges and advantages of working collaboratively, whether that is cross-institution or within your peer group (i.e. teachers). It has necessarily been a whistle-stop tour, as at the time of writing the historical elements of collaboration that were in place for the 14–19 Diploma have been removed and collaboration currently seems to be on a much more inter-institutional rather than cross-phase institution basis. The historical elements, for your information only, can be found in Appendix 2.

References

DfES (2005) *The Education and Skills Implementation Plan.* Nottingham: DfES publications.

Hodgson, A., Spours, K., & Wright S., (2005) *From Collaborative Initiatives to a Coherent 14–19 Phase?* Nuffield Review of 14–19 Education and Training.

Oxford English Dictionary (2nd Edition) (1989) Oxford: Oxford University Press.

Further reading

DCSF (2009) *14–19 Partnerships and Planning.* London: DCSF.

DfES (2004) *14–19 Curriculum and Qualifications Reform: Final Report of the Working Group on 14–19 Reform.* London: DfES.

DfES (2006) *Partnership Guidance.* London: DfES.

Higham, J. & Yeomans, D. (2005) *Collaborative Approaches to 14–19 Provision: An Evaluation of the Second Year of the 14–19 Pathfinder Initiative.* London: DfES.

Hodgson, A., Spours, K., & Wright S., (2005) *The Insitutional Dimension of 14–19 Reform in England: 14–19 Collaborative Learning Systems.* Nuffield Review of 14–19 Education and Training Discussion Paper 10.

Senior, L. (2010) *The Essential Guide to Teaching 14–19 Diplomas.* London: Pearson.

12

Information, advice and guidance (IAG) and employability for the 14–19 sector

Learning objectives

After studying this chapter you will be able to:

- define IAG and CIAG;
- identify the IAG standards;
- explain the importance of IAG for the 14–19-year-old learner;
- explore ways in which you as a teacher can support IAG;
- consider the definitions of employability;
- identify employability skills;
- consider how you can develop employability in your classroom.

Introduction

Information, advice and guidance (IAG) refers to the support provided within educational settings to help young people make informed career choices. With the demands young people face in a changing and complex world there is a need for quality information, advice and guidance, which will enable our students to take the right learning and career options so they succeed in life after school or college. As a concept, IAG covers a range of activities and interventions that help young people to become more self-reliant and better able to manage their personal lives and career.

As a process within education IAG is often linked to careers education and as a concept, it is an umbrella term that covers a range of impartial activities and processes that can support choices made by learners, the key elements of which are defined as follows:

- **Information**: information is data and basic factual information conveyed through different media (either printed or via IT) on course opportunities, occupations or support services available to the learner.

- **Advice**: advice involves helping a learner to understand and interpret how the information provided might relate to his or her personal situation. Advice helps learners to understand their abilities and targets and may involve suggestions or options on how to go about a given course of action.

- **Guidance**: guidance aims to support learners to better understand their needs, to confront barriers and to make informed and appropriate choices.

Employability as a concept refers to how employable your learners are after completing their programme of study.

A brief history of IAG

To set the scene for the remainder of this chapter it is useful to take a brief look at the history and historical development of IAG. In April 2008 the responsibility for IAG was removed from the Connexions partnership and devolved to local authorities, and a set of 12 guiding principles were introduced to enable young people to receive impartial, high-quality advice on career choices. These guiding principles can be found in Appendix 3. These principles were followed by the 2009 strategy for IAF, 'Quality, Choice and Aspiration – A Strategy for Young People's Advice and Guidance', which published statutory guidelines and guidance for impartial careers education. The key messages of this were that every child would have a personal tutor in the educational establishment, school or college, and parents and careers would be empowered to take part in the advice given to their children. Within the strategy there was an ambition to deliver careers education up to the age of 18. In addition, it highlighted the development of an employer taskforce that would look at how employers could support IAG through mentoring and work experience.

Learner entitlement under the 2009 IAG strategy

Under the 2009 strategy young people are entitled to the following:

- excellent, personalised and impartial careers information, advice and guidance in schools;
- support for parents to help them help their children make the right decisions;
- online IAG resources, accessible 24/7 by young people and their parents, with links to one-to-one advice;
- opportunities for taster sessions of HE and workplaces to gain a feel for courses and careers;

- opportunities for a mentoring or shadowing relationship;
- access to specialist help for vulnerable young people or those with additional needs.

IAG today

In today's society the future for any young person is likely to be complex and ever changing, with career options becoming more dynamic and demanding higher skill levels. New technologies and changes in social structures mean that new jobs are being created daily, and the rise in the participation age has also led to different options for our young people.

Activity

Go to the following and watch the short YouTube clip: **http://tinyurl.com/qgvvgeo**
How do you think your subject area may change in the next 5–10 years?
What implications are there for you as a teacher to make your learners 'job ready'?

For the 14–19 learner clips such as the 'Shift happens' one you have just seen, plus the continued advancements in technology, mean that today's young adult faces many different issues and questions when trying to make choices that will support them to live enjoyable, productive and meaningful lives. It is likely that young people will ask their teachers for help in understanding the options available to them in career choice. Such questions often overlap with parts of the curriculum, and the answers to them are frequently bound up with teachers' understanding of their students and their potential. They are also bound up with teachers' own knowledge and experience of the labour market, which in many cases may be very limited outside the education sector. For teachers, this can present challenges in terms of skills and knowledge. Should, for example, an enthusiastic biology student be encouraged to pursue an interest in forensic science? Discussing a subject like this requires knowledge of the labour market, which not all teachers have; but refusing to discuss it may be demotivating for a student whose love of subject is bound up with enthusiasm for a potential career path.

Careers advice and guidance in schools has been the subject of some concerns and many employers have been willing to articulate their concerns about recent policy and practice in this area and to argue that improvements are needed:

> The quality of careers advice in England's schools remains in severe crisis. For 93 out of 100 young people to not feel in possession of the facts they need to make informed choices about their future is a damning indictment. These are some of the biggest decisions young people will ever have to take and they deserve reliable, relevant,

inspirational and high-quality careers advice. It's worrying when young people now have tough decisions to make in light of university fees and the growing range of high-quality vocational routes.

(Katja Hall, Chief Policy Director, CBI, cited in CBI, 2013)

Urgent action is needed from government, business and education in order to build robust bridges into the world of work, address the current expectations gap and avert the threat of a lost generation.

(Kevin Green, Chief Executive, Recruitment and Employment Confederation, cited in CSSA, 2014)

One of the key components of a successful education system is giving young people the chance to make informed decisions about their choice of study and raise their aware-ness of the many pathways that they can take beyond secondary education. Surveys by UK employers and higher education institutions suggest students are not as well prepared as they should be for this transition. Put simply, good careers advice is some-thing that's been sadly relegated to casual conversations and accidental discovery.

*(Steve Holiday, Chief Executive, National Grid, cited on the National Grid website, www.**nationalgrid**.com/uk/)*

So who should support a young person in giving them career advice? Up until very recently there was a clear distinction between the role of the teacher and that of the careers advisor. However, recent changes have led to the distinctions become less clear. Following the Education Act (2011) schools in England have taken on respon-sibility for career guidance. This has further blurred the distinction between the two professions. Until this point careers professionals were typically located outside school in an external partnership organisation. Subsequent to 2011, the co-ordination of career and employability learning has been located in the school and has been delivered through many different processes including employability skills, Personal, Social (and Health) Education (PS(H)E), life skills, transferable skills, and so on. With regard to policy, there are three main terms that have been important in this area:

- *Career guidance* is usually used to describe one-to-one interactions between a career professional and an individual.

- *Career education* describes a progressive curriculum of learning activities which are addressed to the issue of career. In England such a curriculum has most usu-ally been taught by a teacher, often with support from a careers professional.

- *Work-related learning* describes a range of activities which support an individ-ual to learn about work. These include work experience, work shadowing, work simulation, and presentations and other interactions with employers and working people.

The government released new guidance for schools on career guidance and inspiration in March 2015. This replaces the previous version of this guidance

(April 2014). The new version of the guidance is considerably different to the previous version. The changes relate largely to wider changes in the policy environment, including the announcement of new funding for careers and the formation of the new careers and enterprise company. However, there, are also a number of other changes, most notably the introduction of a new section on quality assurance. In general, the new version of the guidance is more detailed and provides clearer guidance than the previous version. The government has also released a new version of the guidance for colleges and sixth forms. This has been revised in a far less substantial way than the guidance for schools.

The role of the teacher in IAG

The non-statutory departmental advice issued by DfE (2014) alongside the revised statutory guidance for schools states that: 'The duty sets no expectations for teachers to advise pupils. However, teachers should know where to signpost pupils to for further support.'

All schools are required to provide a programme of careers education for learners from year 7 to year 11. As part of this requirement all teachers could be asked to provide advice and information on careers in their own specialist subject, advice on 14–19 pathways and study programmes and progression routes into higher education. In addition, part of the strategy is that all young people will be provided with a personal tutor and many teachers may be required to take on this role – they will all be expected to build career routes and further learning opportunities into their subject teaching. This next section will consider some of the roles a teacher could play in IAG and careers advice.

Tutorial roles

A teacher may undertake two types of roles as a tutor: firstly as a pastoral tutor, providing advice and support on where to gain information, secondly as a careers tutor providing advice on types of careers available within any given subject area.

Teaching roles

Teaching roles can either be within the subject, making links between the subject and specific skills and employability skills in that subject area, or career-specific, such as within careers education sessions or PHSE type sessions.

Activity

What types of continuing professional development (CPD) might you need to undertake to ensure that the advice you are providing to your learners is impartial and up to date? You may wish to look at the chapter on CPD to help you to formulate an action plan.

Implications for schools

The statutory guidance sets out what schools must have regard to when carrying out duties relating to career guidance. Three levels of requirement are set out in the guidance.

- The term 'must' denotes something that a school has a legal obligation to do.
- The term 'should' denotes something that a school should have regard to, but which is not a legal obligation.
- The terms 'may' and 'can' are also used within the document to denote things that schools may wish to consider but for which there is no formal expectation.

Within this guidance a number of clear requirements are set out for schools.

- The guidance states that the statutory duty requires governing bodies to 'ensure that all registered pupils at the school are provided with independent careers guidance from year 8 (12–13 year olds) to year 13 (17–18 year olds)'. This duty is further defined by a requirement that the governing body *must* ensure that this guidance is impartial, includes information on a range of education and training options and is in the best interests of the pupils to whom it is given.
- The responsibility assigned to the governing body is reinforced in paragraph 39 which states that schools *must* secure independent guidance that includes the full range of education and training options. This paragraph emphasises that pupils' educational and career choices should be their own and in their best interest and that these choices should be informed by career guidance. It also highlights the importance of providing career guidance in good time before key decision points, particularly highlighting the choice of 16–19 study programme and the education and work choices that follow this.
- Schools can retain in-house arrangements for providing advice and guidance to pupils, these arrangements *must* be combined with advice and guidance from independent and external sources.
- Schools *must* ensure that pupils understand that they are now required to continue in education or training until at least their 18th birthday. In particular schools *must* be clear that this does not mean that young people are required to stay in school and that they should be made aware of the full range of ways in which they can learn or combine working and learning.
- Schools *must* provide relevant information about all pupils to local authority support services. The sharing of data is to enable the provision of support and to allow their participation in education, employment or training to be tracked. However, schools *must not* do this if a pupil over 16 or a parent has asked for their data not to be shared (para. 48–49). Schools also *must* notify

local authorities as soon as possible when a 16 or 17 year old leaves an education or training programme before completion.

■ Students with an Education, Health and Care plan or a 'statement' *must* include a focus on preparing for adulthood (including employment) in this plan. In addition, schools *must* co-operate with local authorities in SEN provision.

The announcement of the new careers company working in collaboration with schools and colleges is also discussed within the new guidance as an important new resource for schools which will support their engagement with careers through the provision of advice and brokerage. The company is linked to the proposal by Lord Young to introduce a 'digital enterprise passport' for young people.

Digital enterprise passport

In March 2015 the Government published Lord Young's work on enterprise in education. The focus of this report is the challenge of young people aspiring towards starting their own business and the skills that this change will require that education needs to recognise.

Embedding enterprise into education

Enterprise in education is much more than the creation of entrepreneurs. It is about motivating young people to succeed and supporting them to develop a more positive attitude to life. This is important in any future profession or vocational activity, and will enable them to make better choices throughout their education, professional and personal lives. It is a key strand of employability and employability skills.

One of the key features of enterprise education and employability is that it can often seem that the teacher is doing less. For example, when it comes to enterprise challenges, teams of students are given a specific problem to solve with a deadline and then have to organise themselves and their time in response to this, then work out their own solutions and present their ideas. In these instances, the role of the teacher is more of a facilitator and/or coach supporting and challenging students.

Developing learners' employability

The UK Commission for Employment and Skills (UKCES) provide the simplest and most accessible definition of employability in terms of skills: 'the skills almost everyone needs to do almost any job'. This is a great definition as far as it goes, although employability is not just about skills, it's also about capabilities or competencies: aptitude, attitude and behaviour.

These skills can further be defined as the transferable skills needed by an individual to make them 'employable'. Along with good technical understanding and subject knowledge, employers often outline a set of skills that they want from an employee. These skills are what they believe will equip the employee to carry out their role to the best of their ability.

Employability depends on your learner's knowledge, skills and attitudes, how they use those assets, and how they present them to employers. It is not the same as subject knowledge, qualifications or specialist experience. A brilliant first degree, a PhD and a list of published papers on your CV may not be enough to secure a position. Learners need to be aware of what employers are looking for *in any employee.* And learners now have to demonstrate that they are employable as a person, a team member and as a contributing member of the employer organisation.

So, what exactly are employers looking for in a potential employee? The following list, whilst not exhaustive, provides some suggestions of personal attributes that an employer will look for in your learner:

- a positive attitude: a 'can do' approach, good work ethic and willingness to learn;
- good personal presentation;
- honesty and integrity;
- reliability;
- timekeeping and personal organisation;
- team-working, collaboration and co-operation;
- flexibility;
- commercial awareness and customer focus.

Skills for employability

In addition to personal attributes employers will also look at an individual's skill base. Skills for employability can be broken down into three distinct areas: communication skills, management skills and team-working skills. Within each section potential employers will be looking to ensure that any potential employee can undertake fundamental tasks.

Communication

Within this sub-set of skills employers will be seeking employees that can read and understand information that is presented to them, listen and ask questions, speak and write coherently and share information with other colleagues. They will also expect your learners to manage information responsibly and be able to think and problem solve.

Managing information responsibly and problem solving

Skills that your learners could be expected to show are to:

- contribute to teams by sharing both information and expertise;
- use appropriate technologies and information systems to collect, gather, and organise information;
- set goals and priorities that will balance work and personal life;
- plan and manage time;
- understand the role of conflict in a group in reaching solutions;
- assess situations and identify potential problems;
- identify the root cause behind a problem.

Activity

How can you as a teacher embed communication skills for employability into your curriculum?

The second sub-set of skills are personal management skills that demonstrate an individual's potential to develop and prosper in any given role. These are linked quite closely to the personal skills within PLTS, and can be developed alongside the PLTS skills.

Personal management skills

1 Demonstrate a positive attitude
- □ Feel good about yourself and be confident
- □ Recognise the good efforts of yourself and others
- □ Take care of your health
- □ Deal with people, problems and situations with honesty, integrity and personal ethics
- □ Show interest, initiative and effort

2 Be responsible
- □ Set goals and priorities, balancing work and personal life
- □ Assess, weigh and manage risk
- □ Be accountable for your actions and the actions of your group
- □ Be socially responsible and contribute to your community

3 Be adaptable
- □ Work independently or as a team player
- □ Multitask
- □ Select and use appropriate tools/technology for a project

    ☐   Adapt to requirements that are changing

    ☐   Be able to respond constructively to change

    ☐   Continuously monitor the success of a project

    ☐   Learn from your mistakes

    ☐   Be innovative and creative when exploring potential solutions

4   Continuously learn

    ☐   Be willing to continuously learn

    ☐   Set own learning goals

    ☐   Plan for learning goals

Teamwork skills

The final set of skills that are identified can again be linked to PLTS skills – these are team-working skills.

1   Work with others

    ☐   Work within group dynamics

    ☐   Be flexible: respect, be open to and supportive of the thoughts, opinions and contributions of others in a group

    ☐   Recognise and respect people's diversity, individual differences and perspectives

    ☐   Accept and provide feedback in a constructive and considerate manner

    ☐   Contribute to a team by sharing information and expertise

    ☐   Lead or support when appropriate, motivating a group for high performance

    ☐   Understand the role of conflict in a group to reach solutions

    ☐   Show interest, motivation, and effort

2   Participate in projects

    ☐   Plan, design, and carry out projects and tasks

    ☐   Define objectives

    ☐   Carry out tasks from start to finish

    ☐   Develop a plan, revise, adjust, implement

    ☐   Work to quality standards

    ☐   Monitor the success of projects and tasks

    ☐   Identify where improvement could occur

As previously discussed in the chapter on personal, learning and thinking skills and functional skills, the key debate for you as the teacher is whether employability skills should be embedded or discrete within the curriculum.

Until fairly recently a clear professional distinction could be drawn between teachers (who addressed the curriculum) and career guidance professionals (who advised on career choices and on the transition to work). However, such distinctions are increasingly difficult to maintain in a clear-cut form. What you learn at school is often gateway knowledge for particular post-secondary courses and consequently for particular occupations. Educational decisions are career decisions, while career decisions have considerable educational implications. Furthermore, there are many skills which teachers and career guidance professionals possess in common, as well as others which are complementary.

Employability and careers advice and guidance is concerned with young people learning about the world of work and the process of supporting this learning has similarities with other kinds of teaching and learning. Amongst other consequences this has meant that there is a substantial overlap between the career guidance profession and teaching.

Non-embedded or discrete employability skills

In this scenario employability skills are provided in discrete sessions and not contextualised within the programme of study. Such sessions may include CV preparation, letter writing and interview preparation. Whilst there is nothing fundamentally wrong with this approach in a school or college it could be argued that, for the learner, creating opportunities to develop these skills is better placed within the subject discipline.

Embedded employability skills

It is my opinion that by far the most effective way to develop our learner's employability skills is to embed employability within the curriculum studied. In that way they are planned and learnt within the discipline context and become an integral part of learning in a relevant and, where possible, a real-world context, offering your learners the opportunity to experiment and reflect upon their employability skills and creating further opportunities to develop those skills. Embedding employability skills should involve as much experiential learning (learning by doing) to make things meaningful. The creation of stronger links between the classroom and the workplace is central to enabling both you and your learners connect with the skills they will need in the future. One of the strategies that can be used is to embed practical projects within the subject area to help learners develop skills.

Activity

There are several pre-prepared resources available online to help you plan for employability within your classroom.
Visit www.skillsworkshop.org/resources/fantasy-job-lesson-plan

1. How could you adapt this lesson plan to contextualise it to your subject area?

Conclusions

The whole concept of careers education, information, advice and guidance is about ensuring that your students are ready for the world of work. As a teacher you have a key role to play in supporting this through effective signposting where appropriate, but more importantly in helping your student gain the skills they will need to make them employable in the future. This chapter has highlighted the skills that employers are looking for in new employees and suggested ways in which you can develop these in your classroom.

References

CBI (2013) *93% of Young People are Not Getting the Careers Information They Need.* www.cbi.org.uk/media-centre/press-releases/2013/11/93-of-young-people-are-not-getting-the-careers-information-they-need-cbi/

CSSA (2014) *Securing our Future Talent: The Roles of Employers and Career Professionals in Providing Career Support to Young People in Schools and Colleges.* www.tony stephens.org.uk/download/xxxx/careers_and_enterprise/Careers Stakeholders Alliance.pdf

Further reading

ACEG (2012) *The ACEG Framework: A Framework for Careers and Work-Related Education.* Available from: www.thecdi.net/write/ACEG_Framework_CWRE.pdf (accessed 14 November 2015).

Hooley, T. (2015) 'Career Guidance and Inspiration in Schools (March 2015)', *Policy Commentary 30.* Careers England.

Hooley, T., Marriott, J. & Sampson, J.P. (2011) *Fostering College and Career Readiness: How Career Development Activities in Schools Impact on Graduation Rates and Students' Life Success.* Derby: International Centre for Guidance Studies, University of Derby.

Hooley, T., Watts, A.G. & Andrews, D. (2015) *Teachers and Careers: The Role of School Teachers in Delivering Career and Employability Learning.* Derby: International Centre for Guidance Studies, University of Derby.

Knight, P. T. & Yorke, M. (2004) *Learning, Curriculum and Employability.* London: Routledge/Falmer.

Senior, L. (2010) *The Essential Guide to Teaching 14–19 Diplomas.* Harlow: Pearson.

Work-related activities

- Student visits to work environments – schools and colleges link with businesses to plan visits and agree learning outcomes. The information and experience gained from the visit is then incorporated into the students' studies.

- A key element of the work-related learning framework, which aims to encourage young people to be more enterprising.

- One or more employers delivering sector-specific information to groups of learners on school, college or employer premises.

- People with industrial or commercial experience providing one-to-one encouragement and support to students and trainees.

- Simulated interviews by people who interview candidates as part of their job – injects reality into job/placement searches.

- Short, job-specific tasks and other hands-on experiences which provide opportunities for students to practice what they have learned in the classroom (e.g. drafting a guide or interpreting a set of financial accounts and preparing a report).

- Increasing numbers of young people take part-time employment at age 16+ – this provides opportunities to learn about taking responsibility, customer and cash handling and health and safety procedures, as well as to gather evidence for building a portfolio, whether for A-levels in vocational subjects, key skills or general records of achievement.

- Students, individually or in teams, working on analysing and or solving business related problems.

- Taster sessions providing insights into the world of work – usually in sector- or industry-based workshops.

- Teams of students taking part in business games and work simulations to resolve complex business-related problems and using role playing, teamwork, decision-making and problem-solving skills.

- A placement with an employer in which a young person carries out a task – or a range of tasks – and duties in much the same way as an employee, with the emphasis on learning from the experience. Work experience provides opportunities for learning about the skills and personal qualities, careers, roles and structures that exist within a workplace or organisation.

■ Learners observing others in real working environments, undertaking tasks and talking to staff to find out more about organisations.

■ Employers lecturing and/or leading discussions with students on school, college or employer premises about the realities of the employment and training environment.

An historical overview of collaboration in the 14–19 arena

The concept of collaboration for 14–19 education was first introduced following the publication of 'The Education and Skills Implementation Plan' (DfES 2005). This document was concerned with the then National Entitlement Curriculum, which the Labour government at the time believed could only be offered through collaborative delivery because no single school would be able to provide the full entitlement. Therefore 14–19 partnerships were seen to be critical in ensuring there was a coherent, locally-owned strategy that could provide the 14–19 entitlement for all young people, meeting local needs and with the buy-in of key partners, for example, employers.

In addition, the document discussed the requirement for schools to work in local partnerships with a range of external providers and stakeholders to meet the needs of their students. As a concept, this method of working collaboratively had been in existence in the British educational system for several years with initiatives such as the 14–19 pathfinders and the Increased Flexibility Programme (IFP).

The 14–19 pathfinder initiative

Pathfinder projects were implemented following the 2002 Green paper '14–19: Extending Opportunities, Raising Standards' and the Government's response '14–19: Opportunity and Excellence'. The pathfinders were designed to examine how schools, colleges and work-based learning providers would implement the Government agenda of flexibility within the 14–19 curriculum. Twenty-five local authorities were included in the first round of pathfinder projects, and a further 14 were successful in the 2003 round. Various initiatives were implemented across the country, for example projects relating to local skills shortages (Derby City Council), and the development of the 14–19 curriculum (Kingswood 14–19 pathfinder project).

Evaluation of the 14–19 pathfinder projects, of which there were 39 across the country, identified, 'the positive impact of the continued development of extensive collaborations' (Higham and Yeomans, 2005) as one of the key findings.

The increased flexibility programme

This programme, introduced in 2002, aimed to 'create enhanced vocational and work-related learning opportunities for 14–16 year olds of all abilities', (DfES 2004) and enabled 14 to 16yearolds to study vocational courses within a post-compulsory setting for part of their school week. The programme was one of the first to embrace widening participation strategies and partnership working.

The DfES evaluation of the project highlighted that students choosing to study in further education colleges as part of their education did so because the course reflected a career interest, and that often the institutions were able to offer more specialised resources and expertise. The conclusion of the project was that partnership working also provided an opportunity for certain students, who may not be suited to school and the learning styles in school, to learn in an alternative environment.

The list below presents an historical overview of collaborative practices in 14-19 education post-2005.

- a home institution/off-site provider agreement or contract;
- robust disciplinary procedures which are shared understood and approved by all partners;
- a progress report which monitors the progress of individual learners against agreed targets;
- an induction procedure with evidence of completion by the individual learner;
- strategies for supporting individual learner need;
- a record of current health and safety policy in line with HSE standards covering 14–16 and 16–19 programmes;
- insurance documentation to cover all learners;
- risk assessments to cover all elements of the programme;
- a risk assessment of individual learners when appropriate;
- a record that all staff involved in learning programmes have been cleared by the Criminal Records Bureau (CRB) for work with children;
- verification that qualifications on offer are listed on Section 96 of the Learning and Skills Act (2000), and can thus be delivered in Key Stage 4 to learners in the 14–16 age group;
- all staff involved in delivery to 14–19 year olds have received training and/or are working towards a qualification in meeting the needs of this age group;
- all staff involved in delivery have received at least basic safeguarding board training appropriate to work with young people aged 14–19;
- there is a designated Child Protection Co-ordinator and policies and procedures in place that fulfil local safeguarding board requirements;

- regular surveys of learner experiences are undertaken;
- there are suitable documentation and procedures for communication between the home institution and provider to demonstrate an ongoing dialogue regarding the progress of the learner.

The focus of these quality assurance arrangements was to check that programmes:

- meet individual learner needs;
- ensure young people are receiving high standards of education and training;
- inform curriculum planning and staff development strategies;
- offer the learner opportunities for progression;
- provide learners with a suitable and safe learning environment.

(Adapted from www.education.gov.uk/consultations/ downloadableDocs/Promoting Achievement, valuing success - a strategy for 14-19 qualifications.pdf)

It could be argued that these principles should still apply today.

Case study: Hull and East Riding partnership – an example of partnership working

The Hull and East Riding partnership has been set up to ensure that the schools work in partnership with a range of external providers from the public, private and voluntary sectors to provide an inclusive curriculum which meets the needs of all learners.

The partnership itself abides by local agreements that all home institutions and providers comply with current Local Authority policies, codes of practices, procedures and guidelines for educational visits and off-site activities, although it is the home institution that has the overall responsibility to ensure that they provide a high-quality learning experience both on-and off-site.

Other aspects of the partnership are that all home institutions and providers have a duty to comply with the Disability Equality Duty and the Race Relations Amendment Act 2000; and all programmes contribute to the delivery of the Every Child Matters outcomes. Each institution or provider is responsible for the quality assurance of its own courses, using its own systems and frameworks for lesson observations, surveys and data analysis, and learner surveys. Also, all data on retention, attendance, achievement and destinations is collated and shared between all partners.

In relation to quality and inspection, information regarding the quality of provision (e.g. OfSTED inspection reports, external verification reports, Student Perception of Course analyses) should be made available by all partners on request and there is a shared responsibility to ensure that areas of weakness are identified and addressed by all partners.

Explore the partnership that is in place within your area. Are the elements similar to those described above or do you have other elements in place. What could be improved?

(Adapted from Senior, 2010)

Funding and commissioning of 14–19 provision: a brief history

In 2010 one of the key changes that took place in 14–19 education was the funding and commissioning, as opposed to allocation, of education for the 14–19 year old age group. A National Commissioning Framework (NCF) was developed to provide support and guidance to all local authorities responsible for commissioning provision, and all provision had to be offered by secure and established partnerships. A new funding bodies was set up, the Young Persons Learning Agency (YPLA), who held the overall budget for provision. The YPLA was established by the Apprenticeships, Skills, Children and Learning Act 2009. On 1 April 2010 it replaced the Learning and Skills Council (LSC), which was the UK's largest non-departmental public. Other statutory powers and duties previously within the remit of the LSC were transferred to the Skills Funding Agency and local authorities in England.

Under the Education Act 2011 the YPLA ceased to exist on 31 March 2012. Some statutory responsibilities reverted to the Secretary of State for Education, while many of the YPLA's functions were transferred to the newly created Education Funding Agency.

For details of current funding for 14–19 education visit:

www.gov.uk/16-to-19-education-funding-allocations

References

DfES (2004) *14–19 Curriculum reforms: Final Report of the Working Group on 14–19 Reforms*. London: DfES.

DfES (2005) *The Education and Skills Implementation Plan*. Nottingham: DfES publications.

Higham & Yeomans (2005) *Collaborative Approaches to 14–19 Provision: An Evaluation of the Second Year of the 14–19 Pathfinder Initiative*. London: DfES.

Senior, L. (2010) *The Essential Guide to Teaching 14–19 Diplomas*. London: Pearson.

3

Guiding principles for the IAG standards

The following table summarises the 12 IAG standards and gives a brief overview of how the standards could be implemented.

TABLE A3.1 IAG standards and their implementation

Standard	Implementation
Young people are informed about how information, advice and guidance services can help them and how to access the services they need.	Provision of impartial advice and signposting to the appropriate advice. Use of different advice and guidance services within the education setting.
Young people receive the information, advice and guidance on personal wellbeing and financial capability issues that they need.	Confidentiality assured. Referral to specialist services where appropriate.
Young people have the information they need to make well-informed and realistic decisions about learning and career options.	Provision of information on a full range of careers, progression routes, the labour markets, pay, university courses and fees. Accessible and timely provision. Impartiality
Information, advice and guidance services promote equality of opportunity, celebrate diversity and challenge stereotypes.	Accessibility and equity for all.
Young people (reflecting the make-up of their communities) are engaged in the design, delivery and evaluation of information, advice and guidance provision.	Peer support groups, peer mentoring and advice.
Parents and carers know how information, advice and guidance services can help their children and know how these services are accessed.	Parents made aware of the range of advice givers.

Information, advice and guidance providers understand their roles and responsibilities.	Collaborative working.
Programmes of career and personal development for young people are planned and provided collaboratively.	Collaborative working.
Staff providing information, advice and guidance are appropriately qualified, work to relevant professional standards and receive continuing professional development.	CPD and staffing need audits.
Information, advice and guidance services are regularly and systematically monitored, reviewed and evaluated, and actions are taken to improve services in response to the findings.	Feedback mechanism in place.
Processes for commissioning impartial information, advice and guidance services are effective and result in services that meet the needs of parents/carers and young people.	Arrangements made to ensure that all provision meets the needs of the young person.

(Adapted from DCSF:2008)

Reference

DCSF (2008) *Quality Standards for Young People's Information, Advice and Guidance.* webarchive.nationalarchives.gov.uk/20100418065544/dcsf.gov.uk/everychild matters/resources-and-practice/ig00253/s

Index